The Last Self-Help Book You'll Ever Need

The Last
Self-Help Book
You'll Ever Need

Repress Your Anger,

Think Negatively,

Be a Good Blamer,

and Throttle Your Inner Child

PAUL PEARSALL, PH.D.

BASIC
BOOKS

A Member of the Perseus Books Group
New York

Hardcover published in 2005 by Basic Books
A Member of the Perseus Books Group
Paperback published in 2006 by Basic Books

Basic Books are available at special discounts for
bulk purchases in the United States by corporations, institutions,
and other organizations. For more information, please contact the
Special Markets Department at the Perseus Books Group,
11 Cambridge Center, Cambridge, MA 02142; or call (617) 252-5298 or
(800) 255-1514; or e-mail special.markets@perseusbooks.com.

Designed by Brent Wilcox

Library of Congress Cataloging-in-Publication Data
Pearsall, Paul.
    The last self-help book you'll ever need : repress your anger,
think negatively, be a good blamer, and throttle your inner child /
Paul Pearsall.
        p.   cm.
    Includes bibliographical references and index.
    ISBN-13: 978-0-465-05486-2
    ISBN-10: 0-465-05486-2
    1. Psychology—Popular works—History—20th century.   2. Self-help
techniques.   I. Title.

    BF145.P43 2005
    158.1--dc22
                                                        2005001005

Paperback ISBN-13: 978-0-465-05487-9
Paperback ISBN-10: 0-465-05487-0

10   9   8   7   6   5   4   3   2   1

With aloha
for my wife, Celest, my sons, Scott and Roger,
my mother, Carol,
and in loving memory of my father, Frank

Contents

Acknowledgments

There are few better examples of the limits of "personal power" than writing a book. Without the *inter*personal power of the love of my wife, Celest, and my sons, Scott and Roger, I would not be alive to write this one. Without the wonderfully chaotic family life forged by my mother, Carol, and my late father, Frank, whose spirit still enlivens my soul, my brother, Dennis, and I would not have grown to realize that "us-help" always trumps self-help. Without the aloha of my entire Hawaiian *ohana* (family) *Kuhai Halau O Kawaikapuokalani Pa Olapa Kahiko* and its totally selfless way of living, loving, and working, I may never have fully understood the ancient wisdom of oceanic thinking, which renders the ideas of self-fulfillment absurd. In Hawaiian, I say *"o wau iho no,"* meaning "I express my loving sincere appreciation" to all of you.

I was afraid this book might never find its way to shelves. Because it takes exactly the opposite view of the ideas that sell millions of books, the famous authors who write them, and the popular psychology that has become the new religion in the United States, I wondered whether any publisher would take the risk of challenging the powerful self-help industry. I had almost given up on submitting the manuscript to a publisher when the daring Jane Dystel and her colleagues Jessica Papin and Michael Bourret at Dystel & Goderich Literary Management came to my rescue. When the scientifically skeptical editor Jo Ann Miller of Basic Books expressed her eagerness to jump into the fray with me in questioning the platitudes of pop psychology, I was honored and thrilled. When I met with Basic Books' Ellen Garrison in Hawaii following my address to the American Psychological Association's annual meeting, I could see that her enthusiasm for the project would translate into thorough editing that would help craft the final product. I owe an enduring debt to all these courageous people. I hope all of you are as proud of this book as I am of you.

There are too many others to name here to whom I also owe a profound debt of gratitude. All the scientists whose research I quote in this book have toiled for hundreds of hours, largely in anonymity, to present research-based paths to well-being. Their work is usually found in journals rather than on the self-help shelves, and is presented at scientific meetings rather than on television talk shows; but if we pay attention to what they have discovered and how they approach the mysteries of the human mind, we can find not only valid answers to our questions but also enlightening *new* questions to ask. I have simplified their work to make it accessible to a wide audience, and I apologize for any errors caused in that process.

I have learned much from all of you, but perhaps most of all I've learned that I was right in the central premises of this book. None of us can really ever help ourselves. The real power is not personal but interpersonal. *The* good life is an illusion, but a shared good one is ours for the having when we realize that our problems and strengths do not rest within us. They resonate between us.

Paul Pearsall, Ph.D.
Honolulu, Hawaii, 2005

A Science of Well-Being

*Life used to be so simple before we all
started reading about how to live it.*

BEN WYLD

SELF-HELPLESS

Sixteen years ago, I was gravely ill with Stage IV lymphoma. I feared I
was going to die, my doctors thought I would, and my family did all
they could to avoid accepting that I would. In a clinical sense, I did
"die"; my vital signs were so weak that life was barely sustained.

Like many critically ill people, I panicked. I wanted a sure guide, a
plan for healing, a way to help myself both physically and mentally.
Even though I had been a scientist and clinical psychologist for almost
twenty years, the terror of my illness caused me to seek the kind of certainty that scientifically based psychology seldom offers. I wanted
something—anything—that could help me retain control of my destiny.
I abandoned my scientific thinking in favor of slickly packaged

1

promises and programs that offered exactly what I wanted to hear. I entered the world of self-help.

The seductiveness of self-help books appealed not just to me but to my friends and family, all of whom were desperate to help me. Almost every day, I was presented with another new program or technique, and I ended up with more than fifty half-read how-to-heal books and tapes shoved under my bed, each to be displayed when the person who sent it visited. The books actually began to interfere with the operation of my hospital bed.

But strangely, the more self-help ideas I was given when I was sick, the more pressured and helpless I began to feel. *What's wrong with me?* I wondered. All this tried-and-true wisdom and I can't benefit from it? Why did the philosophy behind self-help seem so obvious to everyone but me? With all the pain and death surrounding me on the cancer ward, the prescriptions for a positive attitude, for mind over matter, and for unwavering hope began to ring hollow and to feel almost sacrilegious. The self-help mantras were failing to provide the three things I needed most: meaning, comprehension, and management. Traditional psychology has shown that this is what constitutes the sense of coherence essential to real self-help.[1] Why couldn't I do what millions of self-helpers said they did? Was I a self-help failure?

When a nurse said, "These books are really getting in the way," the metaphor was not lost on me.

FAST FOOD FOR THE HUNGRY SOUL

The self-help genre is based on applying sound psychological principles to our daily lives—based, in other words, on science. But in recent years it has become its own industry, dislodging itself from that firm anchor. Research-based psychology is being ignored. Psychotherapy is now almost exclusively for those who are "really sick," and self-help serves the masses of "worried well" as a psycho-morality of living, loving, and working. We are all looking for the "good life," but we have become psychologically myopic. The tenets of self-help are now so ubiquitous that they are no longer questioned: Everyone—from politicians and professors, from teachers to talk-show hosts—parrots the platitudes of self-empowerment as if they were every bit as scientifically tested as the laws of physics. But, as I will show, they are not only wrong, they are harmful. The unsubstantiated prescriptions, programs, guarantees, and gurus of self-help stand in the way of our fulfilling our true potential for satisfaction and happiness.

I present a "Facts of Life" test to audiences made up of people who voraciously consume self-help books. I've collected their answers over the years; I've also given the test to researchers in psychology, psychiatry, and medicine so that they can compare their answers to those of the average self-help reader. Their answers are revealing. Try it yourself, and then I'll explain.

The test is only twenty questions; check statements that you think lead to a healthy, happy life:

1. ____ We must never lose hope.
2. ____ We should be forgiving and never judgmental.
3. ____ Childhood experiences determine adult feelings and behavior.
4. ____ True love should be unconditional.
5. ____ A positive attitude heals and a negative attitude can make you sick.
6. ____ Winners never quit and quitters never win.
7. ____ High self-esteem is essential to mental health.
8. ____ Grief counseling is helpful for major life losses.
9. ____ Living in denial is unhealthy.
10. ____ Most people are addicted to something.
11. ____ Being in "recovery" from an addiction is a lifelong process.
12. ____ Regular vigorous exercise is essential for a long life.

13. ____   If you pick the right diet and have enough willpower, you will be the weight you want to be.

14. ____   Most people with heart disease risk factors such as obesity, high blood pressure, and addiction to smoking will eventually have a heart attack or stroke, and most people who have none of the known heart disease risk factors will not have a heart attack or stroke.

15. ____   You have unlimited personal power. If you want something badly enough and put your mind to it, you can achieve it.

16. ____   You can't love someone else until you first learn to love yourself.

17. ____   Being codependent is a sign of personal weakness.

18. ____   We must get in touch with our feelings and act on them.

19. ____   Feeling guilt and shame is unhealthy.

20. ____   Lasting relationships require a lot of verbal communication.

The average score on this test was 18, and nearly half of those who took the test agreed with all twenty statements. But what if the exact opposite of each of these statements were true? This book presents solid research evidence that suggests that this is so. The best score should in fact be 0! And, indeed, twenty researchers from the fields of psychology, psychiatry, and medicine all scored exactly that.

QUESTIONING THE "FACTS"

Begin by asking yourself these crucial questions:

Do You Really Feel That Worthless? The starting point of self-help is the conviction that we need it. That we are afflicted with an epidemic of low self-regard is widely discussed and widely accepted. Melody Beattie, the author of the mega-seller *Codependent No More,* wrote, "We all suffer from that vague but penetrating affliction, low self-worth." Her advice? "Stop torturing ourselves, start raising our view of ourselves, and right now, give ourselves a big emotional and mental hug." Surely Ms. Beattie uses the inclusive second person "we" out of compassionate solidarity, because if her program works, she must now totally and completely adore herself.

My book suggests that most of us don't really think all that badly of ourselves in the first place, unless, of course, someone keeps nagging us that we should. In fact, most of the problems we think we have stem from too much self-focus rather than too little. I've found that the best cure for hypochondria is to take a patient's mind off his own wellness and direct it to someone else's.

Is Self-Esteem Really the Gold Standard of Mental Health? An extension of the "low self-worth" assumption, enhancing self-esteem has become one of self-help's greatest and grandest goals. As expressed by Matthew McKay in his book *Self-Esteem*, "Self-esteem is essential for psychological survival." McKay offered no proof of any kind to support this statement. Although having a decent opinion of oneself is no doubt important, research shows that high self-esteem relates to health problems and stress. Moreover, mass murderers, gang leaders, and even playground bullies are distinguishable not by their low opinion of themselves (the low opinion that is alleged to lead them to prove their worth through violence) but instead by their inflated self-esteem and disregard for others.

Must You Love Yourself Before You Can Love Another? Another of the central assumptions of the self-help movement holds that before having any sort of romantic relationship, you must first learn to love yourself. As Whitney Houston asserted in the song that has become a veritable self-help anthem, "Learning to love yourself is the greatest love of all." In his best-seller *Love 101: To Love Oneself Is the Beginning of a Lifelong Romance*, Peter McWilliams asked, "Who else knows what you want, precisely when you want it, and is always around to supply it?" His answer? "You!" Melody Beattie's *Have a Love Affair with Yourself* contains the same message. In her best-seller *Letting Go of Stress*, self-help guru and personal-power retreat leader Jackie Schwartz gave this advice: "Write a love letter to yourself and tell yourself all the attributes you cherish about yourself, the things that really please, comfort, and excite you." My book holds that the opposite is true, that loving others makes us more love-worthy and lovable and presents research that demonstrates the importance of loving others first.

Is Being Judgmental Bad for You? Graduates of self-help schooling must not only be in perpetual self-enhancement mode, they also must be nonjudgmental. *Self-Esteem* author Matthew McKay wrote, "You must give up your opinions about the actions of others. Don't make moral judgments. People are doing the best they can." As with all self-help premises, there is a kernel of truth about the importance of avoiding snap judgments, but I argue that making moral judgments about others and ourselves is essential to mental and social well-being as well as spiritual and moral growth.

Is It Harmful to Feel Guilty or to Worry? In *Your Erroneous Zones,* Wayne Dyer called guilt and worry "useless, unnatural emotions." He wrote, without a shred of research support, "You can look at your guilt either as reactions to leftover imposed standards in which you are still trying to please an absent authority figure, or as the result of trying to live up to self-imposed standards. In either case, it is stupid, and more important, useless behavior." I beg to differ. Guilt and worry are natural and necessary evolutionary responses. If our ancestors had not had them, we wouldn't be here today. Vigilance for what might go wrong and reflection about what did go wrong allowed our ancestors to survive. This book challenges this self-help philosophy and presents evidence that the happiest, healthiest people are, in fact, guilty worriers.

So why is it that fallacious ideas have been so widely and willingly accepted? First, I suspect, because academic psychology, with its focus on pathology, has not been much help to people meeting the challenges of everyday life. Moreover, these days, Freud's goal of "normal neurosis" doesn't appeal to us. We want to be free of neurosis.

We're looking for ways to cure ourselves of pervasive feelings of un-happiness, the sense that we are languishing despite all our advan-tages. In 1995, the Midlife in the United States Study surveyed a representative sample of 3,032 adults between the ages of twenty-five and seventy-four. Conducted by an interdisciplinary team of scholars (supported by the John D. and Catherine T. MacArthur Foundation) who studied healthy aging and human development, it found that fewer than two in ten adults were flourishing, that is, feeling and doing well every day.[2] The study was widely reported in the press be-cause it reflected a malaise most of us have felt: Our lives may be peaceful, we may have material advantages undreamed of by much of the world, yet we continue to exist in a state of discontent. We do not, to use a word popularized by the psychologists Fred B. Bryant and Joseph Veroff, *savor* our lives.

I believe that this languishing, this absence of savoring, even more than disasters such as illness, death, and divorce, is what drives flocks of seekers to the self-help section of the bookstore. We're all looking for ways to savor our lives, ways to shake off that languor and begin to thrive. The culture of celebrity that has sprung up around such people as Dr. Phil and Dr. Laura, Deepak Chopra and Tony Robbins, thrives on the vibrancy that these gurus radiate and is perpetuated by the un-questioning faith of their followers. They seem to hold the key to The Good Life, and we've become a society of contentment consumers who are too busy, too distracted, or too self-absorbed to look carefully at what they're offering.

"Positive psychology" is a branch of psychology that asks how we can flourish and what we can learn from those who exhibit resilience and genuine happiness. And what the real science of positive psychology tells us—that The Good Life is a myth—contradicts one of the most sacred shibboleths of self-help. What we each need to find is A Good Life. No plan laid out in a diet book, sex guide, or relationship manual is going to help us find it.

THE GOOD NEWS

Much of the current self-help movement offers comforting and fun ideas, but the glare of celebrity and the seduction of simplicity have blinded us to the science that can make these ideas work. There's a parallel self-help universe out there that many of us are failing to see. It's made up of lessons learned not just by personal experience and anecdotes but also by hard-nosed scientific psychological research.

The good news about self-help and pop psychology is that much of what it has produced could, in fact, be very helpful, but only if we are more mindful of its premises, if we question those premises, and if we compare them with the results of scientific research. Self-help without science is like a beautifully decorated home with no infrastructure. Sooner or later the roof will cave in and those carefully arranged curtains will be buried in rubble. But attention to the facts supporting self-help proclamations could—to borrow a popular self-helpism—*empower* some of pop psychology's prescriptions, and allow them to become more than window dressing.

I wrote this book to offer a practical lens through which to view the candy-colored world of self-help. I don't suggest that you throw your old books away, nor do I advocate abandoning self-improvement altogether. My hope is that those books will become *more* useful after you finish reading this one. Real self-help requires an appreciation of both sides of the psychology universe—the scientific and the popular—and a constant questioning of the "facts." Only then can we begin to flourish and find *a*, not *the*, Good Life.

PART I

Why Self-Help Hasn't Helped

"They say where there's a will, there's a way.
Well, I've got the will. It's finding
the way that's the hard part."

CANCER PATIENT

Self-Help Needs Our Help

*It is the mark of an educated man to be able
to evaluate a thought without accepting it.*

ARISTOTLE

JANUARY 1 IS "Self-Help Day." On the first day of the New Year,
millions of people try again to be better than they are. I've done it
myself, but no matter what I promised myself—that I'd eat better food,
exercise more, meditate daily, or become more organized—I ended up
a self-help failure. When I began researching the self-help movement a
few years ago, I resolved to stop making New Year's resolutions to improve myself, but I failed.

I've been well indoctrinated by the self-help tomes that clog bookstore shelves. I've been guilty of taking up some of that space with my
own, and I hope that this book won't be seen as another *Stop Buying
Other Self-Help Books and Just Buy Mine*. I'm hoping instead that
you'll find its challenges and research worthy of your consideration and
that you will come away with an informed opinion about the advice
you want.

FIND A PITCH AND PULP IT

I recently read Al Franken's *I'm Good Enough, I'm Smart Enough, and Doggone It, People Like Me!*, which pokes fun at the idea that we are all so flawed, miserable, and insufficiently loved that we need help. The industry that perpetuates this idea generates millions of dollars through books, tapes, seminars, and television commercials by exploiting the "find a pitch and pulp it" principle. Just come up with an idea that appeals to the public's nagging sense of needing help, find a clever phrase to describe the approach, develop a multistep guaranteed program, and write it up in an inspirational and authoritative style. Then all you have to do is publish it, promote it through seminars and retreats, and, most of all, promote yourself.

Are we dependent on the teachings of self-help because we are more troubled than our great-grandparents were? I don't think so. I think we've become more self-centered and our expectations have risen to unrealistic heights. With most of our basic needs met, we have the time to think about new ones. Most of us have enough money to "go for more" (self-help books aren't written for the poor), and instead of trusting our intuition or relying on older and wiser friends and relatives, we turn to strangers who offer catchy twists on ways to the good life.

THE SELLING OF SILLINESS

Millions of people buy some kind of self-empowerment book every year. The United States may be the leader of the self-help gurutocracy (more than 20,000 self-help titles are currently listed on Amazon.com), but other countries also have their share of self-help seekers. For example, even independence-loving Australians shelled out more than $24 million last year for books telling them how to live.

Voices shout from the ever-growing self-help shelves. They tell us how to improve our diet and exercise regimens; how to grow our bank balances; how to manage our hormonal balances; how to advance our careers; how to develop a relationship with God; how to conquer our fears; how to improve our sex lives, family lives, and private lives. They tell women how to be more like men; they tell men how to tap their feminine side—and some even claim that men and women are from different planets. They call to children, to the elderly, to ethnic minorities, and to every conceivable sexual orientation. They even give self-help advice to pets.

But look around. Americans are still fat, unhappy, and lovelorn. We are spiritually adrift and our dogs don't behave. Despite the hundreds of guaranteed programs designed to help us discover our full potential and lead wonderful lives, most of us still languish in the doldrums or think we're not as happy as we should be. The self-help market is flourishing, not consumers. The American Self-Help Clearing House in Denville, New Jersey, lists more than 1,000 international self-help groups, and it is estimated that at least one in five people have participated in some form of self-help program.[1] The market thrives on instability. After all, without insecurity, without doubt and unhappiness, where would the self-help industry be? Despite our best efforts, self-help just hasn't helped. As the farcical book *God Is My Broker* asserts, "The only way to get rich from a self-help book is to write one."

But there's hope for the future of self-help. Instead of growing angry with the self-help movement, I have gained a different and deeper appreciation for it as a system not to direct us but to guide and challenge us. It can help us develop healthier minds and bodies, but only if we think clearly about its ideas and then create our own. In the following chapters I offer suggestions for how the science of psychology and the wisdom of lived experience can offer structure to the confusing world of self-help. But before we can know where we're going, it helps to look back at where we've been.

THE FATHERS OF SELF-HELP

Self-help is hardly new. The first such book, called *Self-Help*, was writ-ten in 1859 by a Scottish author, physician, and social reformer named Samuel Smiles. The first sentence read: "Heaven helps those who help themselves." Smiles also wrote, "Hope is the companion of power, and mother of success; for who so hopes strongly has within him the gift of miracles."[2] If he were alive today, his perfect "positive-attitude" name and his unequivocal, miracle-making optimism would likely earn him a television talk show.

Smiles's book advocated not only unyielding hopefulness but also a "can do" attitude expressed through industrious effort to improve one's self. He wrote, "'Where there is a will there is a way' is an old and true saying. He who resolves upon doing a thing, by that very resolution, often scales the barriers to it, and secures its achievement. To think we are able, is almost to be so. To determine upon attainment is frequently attainment itself."[3] Or, in today's jargon—Just Do It!

The ethic of the good life—and the power of positive thinking as the way to it—was also preached by a clockmaker named Phineas Parkhurst Quimby. Born in 1802 in Lebanon, New Hampshire, "Park" is considered to be the father of "New Thought," a mixture of the power of the individual mind, pseudoscientific assertions, various an-cient healing systems, and a kind of secular church of the sacred self. Some see Park's philosophy as a precursor to "new age" thinking.

Although he had no formal training, Quimby had the prerequisite in-spiring personal story to tell. He developed tuberculosis as a young man but became disillusioned with the standard medical treatment of the time. He abandoned traditional medicine and pursued a self-healing approach, which, for him, meant going for long carriage rides. After studying various healing methods, he became convinced that "rightful thinking heals."[4]

Like many self-help celebrities, Quimby eventually opened his own treatment center. One of his followers, Horatio W. Dresser, even offered a "seven element list" for healing that was based on Quimby's teachings; like many current seven-step programs, Dresser's list included religious references.[5] Quimby either didn't take his own advice or didn't succeed at it because it failed him; he suffered from chronic bad health in his later years and died at sixty-four from what today's self-helpers might diagnose as "workaholism."

In 1952, nearly a hundred years after Dr. Smiles and Mr. Quimby, Norman Vincent Peale published *The Power of Positive Thought*, a self-help classic that he based on Christianized self-esteem and revivalist enthusiasm. Still published today as *The Power of Positive Thinking*, Peale's book promised that "enthusiasm makes the difference" and the "positive principle" will show us how to have the good life. He promoted ideas that began with Quimby and Smiles: Never give up hope, cultivate high and ever-elevating self-esteem, always have a positive attitude and positive thoughts, disease is caused by wrongful thinking or a bad attitude, we can succeed through mind control, and the good life is ours for the taking if we want it badly enough.[6] Peale's positive-thinking book has sold more than 7 million copies and has been translated into several languages.

DONAHUE, DR. RUTH,
AND THE KINSEY INSTITUTE

"You've got to get on Phil Donahue." That's what I was told after my first book was published. "That's the only way you get a best-seller," said one publicist. "Phil's the guy everyone turns to for the best advice about life issues. He's the one who can make your book a best-seller." It was the early 1980s, and I was chief of an outpatient psychiatric clinic in Detroit that addressed the problems of daily living. My patients often came armed with self-help books and talked about the latest life-living wisdom as preached by an expert who had appeared on Donahue. Donahue was then what Oprah and Dr. Phil are now: the arbiter of how life was to be led, or at least of who gets to teach it.

On a recent visit to New York, I picked up the latest issue of the Learning Annex's list of courses for personal growth. This pamphlet contains dozens of classes designed for a society that never fully grows and matures. Immanuel Kant wrote that enlightenment is man's emergence from his self-incurred immaturity and that immaturity is the inability to use one's own understanding without direction from another. If he was right, the classes in the Learning Annex's school should appeal to what has become our perpetual childish dependence on others' ideas of how and why to live.

Students shopping for growth at the Learning Annex are offered Deepak Chopra's "secrets of healing, love, compassion, faith, and who we truly are," taught in three hours for a fee of $150 that includes a reception at which Chopra himself will appear. Once they have attained all the healing, love, compassion, and faith they need, they can then sign up for "a day with John Bradshaw" on "how to create healthy loving relationships in every part of life." The fee is only $99.95, but it, too, includes a VIP reception. And if your life isn't too swell on this side of heaven, you can buy a day with "renowned spiritual medium and healer Rosemary Altea based on her latest book" and learn about "soul signs and how to make contact with the other side." You can be taught by "renowned and wildly popular sex educator Dr. Sue Johnson" how to find not just love but "mad passionate love." You can also learn the art of schmoozing, how to communicate with the angels, and how to go to "dream school for big kids."

There is probably some valid information to be gleaned from the Annex's many programs, but helping yourself to it isn't easy. Every course offers the ultimate solution to whatever ails you—and often for what doesn't ail you but should—so perhaps a course on how to do the Learning Annex should be offered.

THE GURUTOCRACY ELITE

While Smiles, Quimby, Peale, and the gurus of the Learning Annex were writing "for the people," academic psychology remained firmly entrenched in its ivory tower. The mysteries of the mind remained impenetrable to most, and wisdom was granted only to a select few after years of study. Mental health care, like physical health care, was available to those with the means to pay for it, and, what's more, psychology's practitioners became ever more rarified in their interests. Rather than offer solutions to life's quotidian problems, many academic psychologists preferred to investigate exotic illnesses, dark Freudian secrets, and bizarre behavior. In its availability and its practicality, psychology was becoming inaccessible to the average person. No wonder Dr. Smiles and his descendants seized the opportunity to fill the gap.

Smiles and Quimby were successful authors in their time, but they achieved nothing like the first-name celebrity status our self-help gurus are granted today. Oprah and Deepak, Dr. Phil, Dr. Laura, and Dr. Ruth are familiar names in most households; indeed, their authority on matters of the soul, mind, and body depends on that name recognition. How many of Dr. Laura's listeners know that her doctorate is actually in physiology, not psychology; that Dr. Phil's education in psychology did not include specialized training about diet, marriage, sex, and parenting; that Dr. Ruth's degree is in education and that most of her advice in matters sexual is purely her own opinion; or that Dr. Chopra's training was in endocrinology, not in spirituality, love, business management, quantum physics, and all the other areas in which he offers his secrets of the good life?

The power of celebrity is supreme in our culture. As the influence of the major self-help gurus shows, celebrity stems more often from media savvy than from scientific expertise. Of the many brilliant researchers, thoughtful scientists, and wise therapists in the world, few have the publicity skills or camera-friendly features of the self-help sensations. They're busy teaching at universities and publishing in academic journals; they are not on the faculty of the Learning Annex or writing self-help books. They were not on Donahue, they do not appear on Oprah, you won't hear about them on Laura's radio show, and you won't see them on Dr. Phil. But you will read about their work in this book.

THE TONO-BUNGAY EFFECT

What happens when a seductive self-promoter meets a celebrity-worshipping society? One answer can be found in H. G. Wells's *Tono-Bungay* (1909). Though less famous than *War of the Worlds* and *The Time Machine*, *Tono-Bungay* met immediate acclaim as a classic depiction of chicanery and credulity. Wells describes how Edward Ponderovo finds fame and fortune with his bogus—but masterfully marketed—cure-all elixir called *Tono-Bungay*. (Whether intended or not, "Tono-Bungay" sounds to the modern ear a bit like "total bullshit," reflecting the true nature of Edward's worthless but well-marketed snake oil.) The stuff is eagerly purchased and swallowed by members of a distracted and needy society in the early 1900s because they have been convinced they could have a better life, yet they are too busy to find it for themselves. Combining science and social satire, Wells describes how salesmanship can triumph over substance and what happens when our discontent causes us to become eager consumers rather than careful contemplators. Failing to examine the reasons for their discontent and then seek solutions, Edward's followers blindly put their trust in a worthless product.

In an early version of a public relations campaign, Edward teaches his young nephew how to market the elixir: "Shout it loud! Tell every one. Tono—TONO—TONO-BUNGAY!" We are shouted at today by pop psych pitch people and their publicists; no matter how smart we think we are, it's difficult to resist the seduction of self-helpism when it appears to offer so much, so fast, and so certainly.

Edward used his credentials as a pharmacist to add prestige to his claims. Had he lived today, he might well have persuaded us to swallow his Tono-Bungay because he could have reached millions who are willing to defer to an authority achieved primarily through declaration. His modern-day counterparts invade our consciousness and define the good life for us, show us how to have it, and provide cures for whatever is preventing us from living life the way they say it should be lived. Sadly, Wells's views of how gullible, compliant, and corrupted society is are as relevant today as they were when *Tono-Bungay* was written.

CLOSED MIND, OPEN WALLET

"The Tono-Bungay effect," then, refers to the mass unquestioning acceptance of an assertion about well-being that is based on the fame and marketing skills of its promoter. The Tono-Bungay effect is best exemplified by our acquiescence with the self-help movement's assertion that the self is everything, that something is wrong with the self, that whatever is wrong is inside the self, and that someone else knows how to fix it.

This form of acceptance—uncritical mob thinking that shouts down skeptics—is what I call "compliant thinking." We are too compliant when we accept the ubiquitous but unsubstantiated platitudes promoting "the good life" that pop up on book shelves, television screens, and magazine covers. Compliant thinking leads to the universal application of certain "facts" (to be addressed later) to nearly every modern ill.

Evidence that we have become a compliant self-help society can be found in our daily language. How often have you heard friends use terms such as "empower," "get in touch," "transcend," "be positive"? How often do you use them yourself? They crop up continuously, but what do they actually convey? A phrase as nebulous as "getting in touch with my inner feelings" is a panacea for a host of ills, not a code to live by. And "be who you are," another mantra from the self-help world, is an instruction so vague that it's impossible to follow. The meanings of these words and phrases are rarely examined; they have been stretched and twisted to become meaningless shorthand for ideas of self-helpism.

LETHAL PLATITUDES

One of the stranger cases I encountered in my practice involved a husband who had always been peaceful but who suddenly turned on his wife one night and beat her terribly. His behavior was so unusual, so inexplicable, that although he was sentenced to jail, his wife decided to bring him in for marital counseling while he was out on bail. When the two came in to meet me, he sat quietly dejected as his wife recounted a several-year history of "self-help" attempts to "save our marriage."

Diane said that she and her husband had attended several "relationship retreats" and tried "marital programs" without success. "We've read the best relationship books, and we watched a TV show about people with damaged inner children marrying one another, but nothing helped. Then," she said, "Harold just snapped. He had never hit me before or even threatened to." At one couples' group, the counselor told her that she had probably failed to see her husband's abusive nature all along because she might have been abused as a child and had repressed her memory of it. The wife added, "I think she was right. I read a book about how you are damned to relive your past even if you don't know you have that past and that your repressed memories can control and even ruin your life. I think it must have been there all the time and that I enabled it for years. It was my low self-esteem that actually ate away at him. I wasn't in touch with my feelings and he wasn't in touch with his. His mind was full of anger, but he wouldn't face it and express it. If you don't get it out, it ends up exploding, and that's what he did."

As I grew increasingly frustrated with Diane's litany, I turned my attention to her husband. I could see that although his head was still, his eyes were darting back and forth oddly. There was a slight tremor in his hands, and when I asked him about it, his wife answered for him. "One of the group leaders saw that, too. She said it was a sign of his trying to hold in his simmering rage."

As a clinical neuropsychologist, I had my doubts about this. I sent Harold in for neurological assessment and a brain scan. The test revealed the presence of an oligodendroglioma, a rare kind of slow-growing brain tumor, located in an area of the brain involved in emotional control. It's the kind of tumor that usually strikes in middle age, but it can be surgically removed if caught in time.

As I sat by the man's bed to share with him the terrible news, he flashed a weak smile through his tears and seemed almost relieved. He said, "I guess my wife was right. I was going out of my mind, but just not the way she thought."

This man's real problem was medical, not psychological. The realization came too late for him, though; he died two months after his condition was diagnosed.

WHO SAYS SO AND HOW DO THEY KNOW?

The tragedy that befell Diane and her husband is an extreme example of what can happen when untested self-helpisms replace scientific investigation. Compliant thinkers take at face value their own emotional responses to people, things, ideas, and even themselves. If they feel it, it must be true. "Go with your gut" is their philosophy; for them, feelings become facts.

Scientific thinking begins with skepticism; it puts ideas to the test, submits those tests to others for their consideration, and is more concerned about asking new questions than offering certain answers. Self-help has flourished because of our failure to ask enough of those who offer it. We don't have to be scientists ourselves, but we can pose questions: "What are your qualifications to assert what you are claiming? How do you know? Where's your data? Who can verify what you're saying?"

Self-help marketers seldom refer to specific studies or use hard data. When they do, they often take astounding liberties with findings and conclusions. "Communication is 90 percent body language and only 10 percent words," said one expert as she touted her book about how to get the edge in a conversation. Another, offering a book on scheduling our time, said, "Ninety percent of our time is wasted on unessential tasks." Really? How do they know these things? What if they're wrong? Are we still to follow their advice?

SCIENCE OR SCIENTISM?

By self-help standards, anyone who "thinks too much" may be seen as not "getting with the program" or as lacking independent self-confidence and assured personal power. Political candidates who appear to be slow-thinking, contemplative, and changeable are not likely to have an easy time getting themselves elected, but these traits are preventative of adaptive wisdom.

No matter what political campaigners claim, "flip-flopping" is indicative of someone capable of creative uncertainty, someone who can change his mind in response to new information. Ours is a complex and dynamic world that requires mental flexibility.

As a researcher, I try to be objective about the ideas I share with my readers, but I have often mistaken *scientism* for science. Scientific thinking is a powerful and helpful way of thinking, but sometimes we have to be open to ideas that are still beyond scientific reach. That doesn't make them right or wrong, just important to think about. What bothers me about celebrity experts is that they're practicing a pop psychology kind of scientism. They claim objectivity and careful observation, but often they observe a phenomenon, subjectively interpret it backwards to their own original point of view, and then give advice based on this closed system. For example, one self-helper said, "I see a lot of you cancer patients getting depressed and losing hope. Cancer is caused by depression and a lack of hopefulness, and that's what I see here on the cancer unit. You have to start thinking more positively."

This kind of thinking infuriated me when I was being treated for cancer. Certainly I understand the desire to find a *reason* for misfortune, because a reason gives us something to work from. If there's a reason for a problem, there's a solution to it. But my cancer had more to do with cells metastasizing than with hope fading. I was enraged that anyone would encourage me to take the painful but all too common way out—by blaming myself—instead of facing the cold, hard, scientific facts.

As I recovered from my illness, I began to see that I had been too narrow-minded. I needed to look again at some of the pop psych advice I'd been given while retaining my scientific way of thinking. Modern advocates of self-help present a restricted way of thinking about problems because their answers are simply one man's or one woman's strongly stated point of view. When I was ill, I came to understand the words of the philosopher Huston Smith: "We have all stumbled into these constricting aspects of our contemporary view. We're all responsible for it."[7]

WITHIN OR BETWEEN?

Self-help experts tend to trace most of life's difficulties to "inside" the person involved rather than "between" all the people concerned. A person-focused approach appeals to us because we have all encountered the feelings, fears, and hopes about which they so fluently and convincingly speak. Who has not encountered at least one bully who ruined our school days or made the trip home a nightmare? It's tempting to believe that the problem lies with that person and has nothing to do with interpersonal dynamics over which we might have some influence. But the answers are not always so simple—and psychology does have equally valid science from which we can also learn when we must deal with the dark side of human conduct.

It doesn't require a Ph.D. to figure out why we behave and feel the way we do. Just open your old introductory psychology textbook. The ideas in that book are well worth our attention when we're trying to understand why we do what we do. Throughout this book, I'll be sharing with you what I call "the classics." These are studies from psychology and other health professions that challenge and expand the assumptions of self-help. More than forty years ago, Stanley Milgram conducted a classic study on the conflict between personal obedience to authority (following orders) and personal morality and behavior (how we treat others). More than thirty years ago, Philip Zimbardo conducted another classic study on the treatment of prisoners. We'll consider the ways these experiments offered challenges to compliant thinking as they revealed the dark recesses of the human psyche and the ways in which we resist our worst impulses.

THE MONSTER BETWEEN

Professor Stanley Milgram, a maverick research psychologist at Yale University, was interested in the justifications offered at the World War II Nuremberg War Crimes Tribunal by those accused of genocide. Their defense was that they were obeying orders and that anyone would have done the same. Had these people become monsters because of some character flaw or deep psychological disorder? Did they suffer from damaged self-esteem or parental abuse? Could it be, Milgram asked, that Adolf Eichmann and his accomplices in the Holocaust were telling the truth—that they had committed atrocities because they were told to?

To find out, Milgram turned not to assumptions and theory but to research. He recruited what he called "teachers" (who were the unknowing subjects of the experiment) to do one hour's work for $4.50. The subjects thought they were taking part in an experiment to study memory and learning, and they were introduced to a stern-looking experimenter wearing a white laboratory jacket who exhibited an air of authority. They were also introduced to a pleasant and friendly cosubject who was also presumably recruited via the same newspaper ad. In fact, the cosubject was an actor who was helping conduct the experiment.

Two slips of paper marked "teacher" were handed to the two subjects, but the actor claimed that his paper said "student." This ploy assured that the subjects would think the assignment was totally random. Both subjects then sat in a chair and were given a sample 45-volt electric shock to illustrate what the "student" would be experiencing in a study to assess the effects of punishment for incorrect responses on learning behavior.

The subject was then instructed by a "scientist" (Milgram or one of his assistants, who was wearing a white lab coat) to read lists of paired words to be learned by the actor subjects and to administer a shock by pressing a button each time the "student" made a mistake. It was understood that the shocks were to be increased by 15 volts in intensity for each mistake he made. The apparatus in front of the "teacher" was labeled from "slight shock" to "danger: severe shock." Because the "student" was in another room, the "teacher" could only hear his responses.

No more real shocks were administered, but the "stern" experimenter was in the room with the "teacher" administering the fake electric shocks. Whenever the "teacher" asked whether he or she should continue to administer the shocks, the experimenter encouraged more of them as "part of the study." Despite the pain they thought they were causing their partner in the experiment, 65 percent of the "teachers" obeyed orders to punish the student to the very end of the fake 450-volt scale, and none of the subjects stopped before reaching 300 volts! If a "teacher" asked who would be responsible for harmful effects, the experimenter gave assurances that he was taking full responsibility. That was enough for them to continue their abuse.

Interestingly, when this same experiment was conducted in a nondescript office building rather than the imposing halls of Yale University, where the first studies were done, the percentage of those who complied with the shocking instructions dropped to 47.5 percent. Again, place and personal interaction with the stern experimenter influenced what took place. When Milgram later wrote about his work, he said, "Stark authority was pitted against the subject's strongest moral imperatives against hurting others, and, with ears ringing with the screams of the victims, authority won more often than not."[8]

This type of research teaches us that "between" matters at least as much as "within." Given a certain situation, any of us might engage in behavior we consider horrendous, not just those with corrupted psychological histories. It's not just "inner children gone mad" that's at the root of bad human conduct, it's interaction between people and place.

But some people don't go along with authority when that authority is wrong. What about the "resisters"—the 35 percent in Milgram's study who refused to comply? What was it that allowed them to transcend the situation and behave morally and independently? Psychology has traditionally focused on what is worst and weakest about us more than what is best and bravest. Are "resisters" simply the benefactors of wonderful parenting, or do they learn to think and behave differently on their own or in ways we don't yet understand?

WHAT KIND OF A PRISON GUARD WOULD YOU BE?

On Sunday, August 17, 1971, nine young men were "mock arrested" in their homes by the Palo Alto police. They were among seventy college students who were willing to earn $15 a day for two weeks serving as subjects in an experiment on prison life. After extensive psychological screening to select only the healthiest and most normal of the group, twenty-four were chosen to be either prisoners or guards.

The "prisoners" were then handcuffed and taken by their fake "guards" to a makeshift prison in the basement of Jordan Hall on the Stanford University campus. Those assigned to be guards were given uniforms and instructed not to use violence, but they had to maintain order at the prison.

Two days later, the "prisoners" staged a mock "revolt." After that uprising, the guards became more and more aggressive and coercive toward the prisoners. They humiliated the prisoners by forcing them to clean the toilets with their bare hands and to act out degrading scenarios. The staff conducting the experiment repeatedly told the "guards" to stop their aggressive and abusive behavior, but at night when the researcher was not present, the abuse escalated. In this study, authority was defied and abuse grew harsher.

Late one night, Christina Maslach, one of the psychologists, walked in on the "experiment." She was closely associated with the person in charge of the study, but reported that she was shocked to see young men dressed in khaki uniforms and wearing reflector glasses to hide their eyes herding a group of prisoners. The prisoners wore shapeless smocks, and their heads were hidden beneath paper bags; their pale trembling legs were encased in heavy chains. Dr. Maslach objected to the experiment and was aware that even the researchers had become numbed to what was happening.

The research was stopped. Dr. Maslach is often described by psychologists today as the hero who put an end to the Stanford experiment. She was a "resister," the kind of person we know less about than people who behave badly.

∾

Both of these experiments surprised their creators. Milgram did not expect nearly as many people to go as far as they did in "shocking" their subject. Zimbardo had no idea that the behavior of his "prison guards" would devolve to such barbaric levels. But it is a foundation of good research to acknowledge unexpected results and to work from curiosity rather than from biased expectations.

I had always agreed with Benjamin Disraeli's idea that we tend to put too much faith in systems and look too little to men and women. That belief is reinforced by another aspect of the experiments, another way in which they offer a challenge to compliant thinking: Some of Milgram's subjects did not administer lethal shocks. And Dr. Maslach, who objected to the mistreatment of the Stanford "prisoners," displayed the same kind of contrarian bravery. It's not easy to stand up to our own impulses—including our impulse to accept authority, whether from a white-coated "doctor" or from a talking head on television.

Something inherent to these situations and interactions was affecting the behavior of the participants, not their individual psyches. Brutal, insensitive abuse has many explanations, and we can understand this sinister side of our characters not by relying on clichés and insufficiently researched assumptions but by examining the evidence produced by scientific research.

Earlier, I mocked Dr. Smiles's simplistic positivism, but when I reread his book, I noticed that he discussed the fundamental importance and responsibility of self-improvement and accountability for fulfilling personal potential not just for our own good but for the good of the world. I saw wisdom in his words: "For the nation is only an aggregate of individual conditions, and civilization itself is but a question of the personal improvement of the men, women, and children of whom society is composed."9 His idea that the worth and strength of a state depend less upon its institutions than the character of the people who compose them resonated with me, yet I saw that we were not really helping ourselves at all. We were too easily deferring to others as guides for who and how to be. A society that valued independent self-help above all had become dependent on "other help."

I'VE HAD MY FILL OF DR. PHIL

While I was writing this book, my wife called me to the television to watch an interview with Dr. Phil. As the current spokesperson for all things psychological, Dr. Phil was being asked by an anchor on CNN to make sense of the horrific accounts of prisoner abuse at Abu Ghraib prison in Iraq. Why had American soldiers behaved so despicably? What should be done? As always, Dr. Phil had an answer. He laid the blame on the parents of the alleged abusers; he said the accused torturers likely "suffered from low self-esteem as children" and that they "had become bullies to compensate for their low self-worth." They were "acting out" and—in Dr. Phil's typical get-tough approach—"they would have to be taken care of," apparently meaning they needed some form of intense reparenting. The same CNN interviewer who had been so quick to challenge political figures nodded in agreement and thanked Dr. Phil for his wisdom.

I was appalled, though not surprised. The interview had encapsulated all the toxic elements of self-helpism: compliant thinking, the primacy of celebrity, the application of "soft science." The Milgram obedience experiment and the Stanford prison guard experiment are eerie precursors of the U.S. military prison scandal at Abu Ghraib in Iraq. We know that the powerful instinct to obey is present in nearly everyone, not just in those with low self-esteem. We know that highly controlled environments organized into hierarchies of the powerful and the powerless can lead to abuses of power, whether or not the powerful had neglectful parents. The science-grounded reasons for the terrible abuses in Iraq are available to a lay public—but Dr. Phil chose not to acknowledge them.

Matt Burg of Yale and Teresa Seeman of UCLA have extensively researched the dynamics of taking advice.[10] Although their focus of these research psychologists was on the possible downsides of receiving advice and support from family members during a crisis—such as cancer—and not with ordinary problems of daily living, their findings help alert us to the danger of "advice submissiveness." Burg and Seeman found that advice and assistance from others can be unhelpful and even distressing. It can induce feelings of guilt for being less than we can be, for being a burden, and for being unable to reciprocate. In other words, help can make us feel helpless. It might even cause us to think that our "inner child" is a future serial killer.

CREATIVE SELF-HELP

In our world of self-help we are being smothered with advice that at best does us little good and may even do great harm. At the most desperate moments of our lives, many of us reach out for help—but choose the wrong kind, the compliant kind.

But the opposite of *compliant* thinking is *creative* thinking. Creative self-help begins with the assumption that self-help has been too focused on the individual, and that *inter*personal rather than personal power holds the most promise for helping us live our lives to the fullest. As the Milgram obedience experiments show, it is the relationship between human beings—between the "teacher" and the "student," between the subject and the "scientist"—that determines our behavior. Our problems don't always lie within us. They evolve between us.

Creative self-help also presents the idea that all our problems are interrelated. When something goes wrong, we search the shelves of the self-help section for a book that addresses our specific problem. Diet books don't typically deal with our sex lives, sex books don't usually deal with our diets, relationship books don't deal with death, and books about dying don't deal with any of these issues. We expect our helpers to give us answers to a specific pressing problem—not to distract us with the rest of our lives.

Unless we take a systematic, inclusive, carefully considered approach to a self-improvement project, self-helpism's ideas about life can become limiting and divisive. One of my clients told me, "I think the worst times in our marriage are when my husband gets on another one of his self-help programs. The second worst time is when he fails at it. And whenever he's busy trying to be all he can be, he forgets about trying to be all we can be."

Perhaps self-help's greatest drawback is that we turn to it when we need help but forget about helping ourselves when things are fine. We are too willing to let others do our thinking for us. Self-help failed me because I stopped thinking and focused on doing. But my family and my colleagues helped "re-mind" me to use the kind of thinking that would eventually help save my life—a creative, contemplative, and mindful approach that tapped psychology and modern medicine for the best they had to offer.

In the next chapter, we'll look at some of the most common myths of self-helpism and use creative self-help to arrive at the truth behind each unresearched assumption. My hope is that after reading this book, you will challenge compliant thinking and self-help advice that depends on acquiescence and go forward to a shared good life.

The Facts of Life?

Grace is given of God, but knowledge is bought in the market.

HUGH COUGH

IN 1902, THOUSANDS of Americans died of pellagra, a disease characterized by the "Four D's": dermatitis, diarrhea, dementia, and eventually death. Because so many houses lacked sanitary bathrooms and adequate sewage removal, health experts of the time assumed the disease was caused by a microorganism and transmitted through direct contact with infected human excrement. But this belief had not been adequately tested and little progress was made in curbing the epidemic. One authority who did not believe that pellagra was caused by human excrement was Surgeon General Joseph Goldberger. His simple empirical test solved the mystery of a devastating illness.

Goldberger resisted looking at the problem from one perspective only; instead, he observed his patients, formed a hypothesis, and tested his own beliefs. He noticed that most pellagra sufferers were also malnourished. The contemporary views on pellagra focused on what came out of people, but Goldberger was increasingly concerned with what went in.

In a study that few university research-protocol committees would approve today, Goldberger took small amounts of feces and urine from two pellagra victims, mixed the samples with flour, and rolled the mixture into tiny dough balls. The surgeon general and his wife then ate them! (My wife tells me that living with a scientist is not always easy, but I hope Goldberger's story puts my often annoying skepticism and the testing of accepted ideas into perspective.) When the doctor and his wife remained pellagra-free, Goldberger decided that his hypothesis was worth further testing. He fed an experimental group of prisoners the diet he believed might be causing the disease, one that was deficient in niacin and protein. Of course, no modern-day ethical scientist would contrive or attempt such an experiment, but Goldberger's skeptical "prove it" mind-set is at the core of the adventurously creative scientific mind.

Goldberger's experiment paid off. Within months, his hypothesis about the real cause of the disease was confirmed. All the prisoners who were fed the niacin- and protein-deficient diet developed pellagra; the control group, prisoners on their usual diet, remained healthy.[1] Had society adopted what almost everyone agreed was the best way to deal with the disease, pellagra would have continued to flourish. It might have been a laudable thing to develop better, cleaner, and more efficient bathrooms, but it would not have dealt with the real cause of the problem.

Beliefs serve an important role in scientific thinking, and denying them can prevent a scientist from being fully aware of the limits his or her own beliefs may be imposing. To move forward with a scientific theory, one must, obviously, believe something; the problem arises when a scientist—or psychologist, or guru, or patient—does not distinguish between "belief" and "fact" and develops a bias in favor of his or her own belief. The mind-closing danger of biased beliefs occurs when we don't know we hold them. Sometimes we have to swallow our pride and engage in clear-eyed analysis. Self-help's dependence on bias can result in the failure to understand and deal with the real problems of our lives.

THE "WIDENING CIRCLE" PHENOMENON

Celebrating a baby's first birthday is a big deal in Hawaii. We celebrate life's good start with baby luaus that are usually held at the beach; hundreds of our neighbors and friends bring food and we all play lots of games. I was attending such an event, this one at a friend's house, when a little girl asked me to play a game of ring toss. One by one, she threw each of her rings far outside the white circle spray-painted on the lawn. Before I could take my turn, she ran to her mother, took the paint can used to make our target from her hand, and painted a new wider circle that included all her scattered rings. "See, Mommy!" she announced, "I got them all in!" As is true with many self-help programs, draw the circle large enough after the fact and the interpretation and self-improvement plan appears to be right on target: We could have "known it all along." As the psychologist David G. Myers pointed out in describing what psychologists call *hindsight bias*, "How easy it is to seem astute when drawing the bull's-eye after the arrow has struck."[2]

An example of the widening circle phenomenon is the "emotional hydraulics" belief that underlies much of the self-help movement. This is the unsubstantiated but widely held view that the things that happen to us are somehow stored inside our consciousness only to play a life-long psychological game of hide-and-seek. To help ourselves, we are supposed to look for these hidden feelings within us and vent them when we find them. The self-helpism "get in touch with your feelings" approach derives from this kind of thinking. When mysterious inside emotions are seen as controlling our lives, a wide circle is drawn for the cause of feelings and behavior that are not in our immediate interaction with another person.

When we see ourselves as an emotional hydraulic machine with building internal pressure that must be released no matter what, we end up as a ventilationist society that feels free to spew emotional waste anywhere to anyone at any time. This view has its origins in Sigmund Freud's dated "dynamic" psychology, a word well suited to the pent-up psychic energy aspect of the hydraulics idea. But seeing repressed emotions as paper set afire in a garbage can and locked away has little research support. And the idea that it benefits us to release those repressed and terrible emotions is equally unsupported by science.

FARFETCHED MEMORIES

Self-help not only assumes that emotional pressures are building and that we need to get in touch with them but also that we buried them there ourselves. Self-help assumes that we hide the bad things that happen and that these repressed memories continue, as Freud suggested, to influence how we feel and behave in the present moment until we finally expose and release them. Borrowing from Plato, it then assumes that our presorted memories are perfectly retained. Research shows that 88 percent of university students believe self-helpism's view that we push negative experiences out of our awareness and tuck them into the unconscious.[3]

People have been tried and convicted because of court and jury acceptance of the "recovered memories" of an adult who suddenly (or sometimes with the encouragement of a counselor) recalls abuse by a family member, teacher, child-care worker, or member of the clergy. Much of the character of our alleged "inner child" is assumed to be composed of a repressed montage of misery that can be elicited by free association and gentle seductive guidance from a self-help expert.

An entire self-help industry emerged based on the belief bias of repressed memories and their accurate retrieval. Books, magazines, and television shows have embraced the value of digging up memories, from the traumatic to the trivial, to explain unhappiness or bad behavior. And their methods of "memory retrieval" are often suspect. For example, the self-help author Wendy Maltz has written several books about sexuality, three of which deal with recovering repressed memories of sexual abuse and incest. Maltz receives almost unanimous rave reviews on the Internet, particularly from those who say they have recovered their own memories of sexual abuse. Maltz's way of assisting the recovery of repressed memories of sexual abuse uses another self-help belief bias about the power of imagery, intuition, and imagination as valid ways of "getting in touch" with those mysterious closeted feelings and buried memories. Maltz wrote: "Spend time imagining that you were sexually abused, *without worrying about accuracy, proving anything, or having your ideas make sense* as you give rein to your imagination, let your intuitions guide your thoughts."[4] (My italics.) The twelve italicized words of Maltz's statement constitute the "dirty dozen" of the self-help approach, but should we accept this fundamental belief bias of self-help?

Elizabeth Loftus is a creative, iconoclastic psychologist and researcher who has conducted classic studies that challenge self-helpism's biases about the nature of our memory. In one study, subjects implanted false memories into their siblings' minds. In another, Loftus provided subjects with booklets containing three written accounts of real childhood experiences provided by family members and one false account of being lost in a shopping mall, what came to be known as the "Lost in the Mall" study. Loftus showed that detailed, carefully constructed, and utterly false recollections were easily accepted as truth.[5] She states: "Repression folklore is . . . partly refuted, partly untested, and partly untestable."[6]

Apart from making personal attacks, the self-help world took little notice of Loftus. The repression-obsession continues unabated today despite the evidence showing that it's an overdiagnosed state. Most researchers who have examined the repressed-memory bias contend that repressing bad events is a rare occurrence, if it happens at all.

Research suggests that our traumatic experiences aren't always banished to the assumed deleted-memory bin. Instead, they can produce life-enriching recollections called "flashbulb memories," vivid recollections of significant events that stay with us forever even if, and often because, they were so horrific.[7] It's as if our brain says, "Hey, take a picture of this. You'll want to remember this forever because it changed everything."

Our memories of the assassination of President Kennedy, the events of September 11, 2001, as well as more intimate moments of tragedy, are "flashbulb" memories and they profoundly affect almost all of us. The terrible event is remembered, not repressed. Sometimes, such memories flash or pop into our minds and cause us to reflect on the meaning of another major transitional life crisis. On the morning after the 9/11 tragedy, the *New York Times* aptly described that terrible day as "one of those moments in which history splits and we define the world as 'before' and 'after.'"

SUPPRESSING THE IDEA OF REPRESSION

If some of the worst events in our lives make for the essential "flashbulb" memories that are fundamental to who we are and how we feel about life, where does this leave the idea of "repressed memories"? If our consciousness is designed to conceal the worst that happens to us, how can we explain the following: A study of sixteen children from five to ten years old who had witnessed their parents being murdered and did not repress the memory but thought about it and clearly recalled it.[8] Although only sixteen subjects participated in this study, they all vividly recalled the terrible events they had witnessed. The number is significant not because of its size but because of the thoroughness and unbiased nature of the study.

- People who keep detailed diaries of their daily lives recall negative events as often as positive ones.[9]

- On a neurological unit in a British hospital during World War II, most of the wounded soldiers did not experience repression of battlefield memories. For the 35 percent of those who did experience varying degrees of amnesia, the condition was traceable to concussions, "pretend" or false amnesia, or other physical injury.[10]

Studies show that Holocaust survivors tend to remember all too well the atrocities they experienced and witnessed.[11] As chief of an outpatient psychiatric clinic at Sinai Hospital in Detroit, I met several of these survivors, and not one reported having forgotten or wanting to forget what had happened. One of my patients showed me the blue tattoo that had been burned into his arm at the concentration camp. When one of my young residents asked whether he would like to have it removed, he answered, "God, no! I will never forget. No one should forget. When you see it, you should not forget. I look at those numbers every day and others do. They help me remember what needs to be remembered so such memories will never be made for anyone again."

Because of stress and other health issues, some traumatic events are sometimes forgotten. Terrible things happen to children, and to ignore an adult's plea for help because of a claimed recovered memory of abuse would be cruel and bad medical and psychological practice. To do so would be "junk skepticism," which is as obstructive to true understanding as junk science. We are obligated to check out these reports, but not to give in to them. The idea that we almost always repress what is worst about our lives and that our recollections of these times are accurate is worthy of continued study, not blind acceptance.

The American Medical, Psychological, and Psychiatric Associations, the British and Australian Psychological Society, and the Canadian Psychiatric Association have worked to try to balance total reliance on the idea of repressed and later recovered memories with sensitivity to the suffering of thousands of persons who may have been abused.

Their shared view of the issue was expressed by the Royal College of Psychiatrists Working Group on Reported Recovered Memories of Child Sexual Abuse: "When memories are 'recovered' after long periods of amnesia, particularly when extraordinary means were used to secure the recovery of memory, there is a high probability that the memories are false."[12]

THE ESTEEMED CONCEPT OF SELF-ESTEEM

Another self-help belief bias is the universally accepted idea that enhancing self-esteem is an essential personal responsibility and the major responsibility of every parent. It's assumed that we owe it to ourselves to feel not just good but very, very good about ourselves. Self-helpism also states that teaching children personal power and enhancing their sense of self-potential is crucial to their later adult success. But these platitudes are worthy of more consideration than we've given them.

High self-esteem can be damaging to you and others around you. Think about it: When someone lacks the faculty for self-criticism, she can run roughshod over another's feelings—or rights—with no remorse. When I read John Dean's *Blind Ambition*, I thought he had given it the wrong title.[13] I thought it should have been called *The Danger of Self-Esteem*. The book was about the fall of President Richard Nixon and the kind of disaster that can happen when self-doubt and personal guilt are absent and self-confident arrogance and a "can do anything attitude" run amuck.

According to self-help expert Nathaniel Brandon, "People who have little or no self-esteem have nothing to contribute to the world."[14] Abraham Lincoln was full of self-doubt, guilt, and insecurities, as was Winston Churchill, who spoke about being followed around by his "black dog" of depression and nagging sense of guilt and self-recrimination. Brandon also makes sweeping claims for the power of self-esteem: In his best-selling book *The Psychology of Self-Esteem,* he stated, "I cannot think of a single psychological problem—from anxiety and depression, to fear of intimacy or of success, to spouse battery or child molestation—that is not traceable to the problem of poor self-esteem."[15]

Here are some of the questions that leading researchers Martin Seligman and David Myers are asking about belief biases:

- Does blunting warranted feelings of failure and anxiety really lead to happier and more capable adults?
- Don't children need to fail or to feel sad, nervous, and angry if they are to know success, joy, contentment, and pleasantness?
- Don't children need practice with the "three D's of dark, down, and disappointed" as much as with the more positive ones?
- What about the "no day without night" argument? Doesn't preventing feeling bad make it more difficult to feel good or to know what feeling good is really like?
- Didn't some of the most successful and happy adults also have childhoods filled with negative events?
- Don't some of the world's most miserable and evil people sometimes come from loving and supportive homes?
- Is the long-standing Freudian assumption of the importance of past history really valid?

GUILT: THE NOBLE EMOTION

According to self-helpers, the ultimate antihappy emotion is guilt. They say we can't be happy when we feel guilty, but I say we can't be really happy if we don't. I believe that happiness is not an insular, individual emotion at all but in fact depends on a collective happiness. When someone feels guilty, often it is because he knows he has punctured that collective happiness and thus cannot enjoy it himself.

Guilt is essential for making real changes. It can lead to a more thoughtful consideration of life, how we lead it, and how we influence other lives. The child who learns not to feel deeply ashamed about hitting a friend might never learn that hitting is wrong, or she might come to view that principle as an authority's arbitrary rule. The spouse who cheats, the person who makes a cutting remark about a friend, the parents who neglect their child—all of them *ought* to feel guilty. Without guilt, we might become at best totally self-absorbed beings, or maybe even sociopaths. As the psychiatrist Willard Gaylin told an interviewer, "All the pop psychologists are misleading people about things like guilt and conscience. Guilt is a noble emotion; the person without it is a monster."[16]

Trying to be guilt-free and have the highest self-esteem leads us into an irresponsible life no matter how successful we are in our careers and social lives. If our ultimate self-help goal is increasing and protecting our self-esteem, we risk preventing ourselves from making necessary substantive changes in our lives.

We have become so consumed with trying to feel good that we are becoming sick and tired of trying too hard to be happy; as a result, we savor life too little. We have failed to recognize the ephemeral nature of happiness and the emotional crash that inevitably comes when we're too high too often for too long. Our compulsive search for happiness has left us adrift in a lonely sea of self-celebration, yet we never quite reach the sunny place we hope is just over the horizon. Isn't it possible that when people do bad things, they *should* have low self-esteem and that high self-regard should be earned through accomplishment? It's even possible that low self-esteem leads to the desire to change and help ourselves.

NEGATIVITY AS STRATEGY, NOT SYMPTOM

The exhortation to be positive, to have hope, is another popular self-helpism. It joins the McMorals of the happiness ethic, emotional hydraulics, and repressed memories, and like them, it can prevent us from fully enjoying life. Being hopeful might be a good idea when we're in trouble, but it is not the only idea. If hope is merely adopting a forced illusion, we have to ask whether illusion is the only way people make an effort to improve their situations.

Hope is usually offered when things are not going well, so I heard a lot about it when I was a cancer patient. It's related to self-help's perpetual optimism, but a careful consideration of optimism asks whether illusion or even an optimistic state of mind is the only one that works when we are in trouble. Is deceiving ourselves with forced positive thoughts really helping us, particularly at times when we need help the most?

Self-helpism is dominated by unyielding self-motivation and fueled by relentless hopeful optimism, and there are many examples of people who have experienced great success by thinking this way. Describing the method of his success at the Chrysler Corporation, Lee Iacocca said, "Decide what you want to achieve, and then work tirelessly to achieve it." But certainly there are people who decided what they wanted to do, worked tirelessly, had a winning attitude, yet still didn't achieve their goals. These people are left with heartbreak, despair, and self-loathing. For every Lee Iacocca, there are a dozen hardworking and highly self-motivated people who consider themselves failures by self-help's standards.

When I was sick, I was constantly encouraged to keep hoping and was given several best-selling books by the celebrity prophets of anti-pessimism who claimed that hope was the one thing we should never give up. To them and to those who gave me their books, "never give up hope" was a fundamental dictate that could not be questioned.

No one gave me a book about the joy of hopelessness, so I had to put my own mind to the issue. The more I thought about hope as being *a* way—but not *the* way—to deal with adversity, the more I also began to find value in giving up hope as a way to think differently about my life, particularly during times of my deepest despair.

I began to fear that constant hoping might cause me to sacrifice today for the illusion of a better tomorrow. I wondered whether I was allowing others to see my present as devoid of meaning. I thought that the future could also be seen as a time that arrived yesterday and passed to today before I had time to think about it. Constant hoping led me into reckless regard for how I was evaluating my own present, a state psychologists call "mindlessness." I've learned that the truly healed mind is wide open to the present and not blinded by promises of a better future.

My own experience leads me to suspect that telling people who are suffering never to lose hope can make them conceal their pessimism or fear. The author of a recent study on hope's relationship to cancer described it as "the misguided belief that this [hope] will afford survival benefits."[17] There is no scientific evidence to show that hope influences therapeutic regimens or prolongs life, though it may help improve the quality of life. But to emphasize only hope can burden patients with expectations they don't need at a time when they are already under extreme stress. As the author of the study on hope points out, "If a patient feels generally pessimistic . . . it is important to acknowledge these feelings as valid and acceptable."[18] In other words, it is as much a part of the healing process to be mindful of our despair as our optimism, for in both rest lessons essential to living and dying well.

It might be helpful to do a little less hoping about the future and pay more attention to life in the present through the full engagement of all our emotions and those of the people around us.

THE ADDICTION FICTION

The concept of addiction is another arm of the self-help good-life trinity. It is the classic method by which we locate the cause of a human failure in external factors. Because of the seductiveness of that proposition, there has been an almost total acceptance of the ideas of addictive personalities, multiple addictions, and even a range of intensity in addictions from soft to hard. We assume we can be addicted to things, behaviors, and people, be they alcohol, work, sex, chocolate, a lover, or television watching. If addiction really existed as self-help says it does, we would be in danger of becoming addicted to addiction.

A Japanese proverb is often quoted in addiction recovery centers: "First the man takes a drink, then the drink takes the man." This statement suggests that addiction is caused by outside forces that we just can't deal with, a view that is unsupported by research. Lots of people take a drink, but few are taken for life by it.

Real addiction tortures souls, ravages bodies, and destroys families. It's important to remember, however, that "addiction," as self-help defines it, is an invention. It doesn't "exist" in the same way that a virus or a bacterium exists. As the maverick addiction researcher Bruce Alexander pointed out, there is no such thing as a substance that causes addiction. Addiction is not a fact of life but a description about how we are choosing to live.[19]

In the 1960s, the physician E. M. Jellineck was one of the first to label alcoholism a disease. This biomedical bias asserts that alcoholism is an inherited tendency toward physical dependence; that is, chronic brain disease is caused by the biological effects of psychoactive drugs and results in withdrawal when the drug is taken away. Self-help translated this view to its own criterion for declaring a behavior to be "addictive." It essentially said that anything you do that is difficult to stop doing is an addiction.

Into the 1970s, the disease bias was supported by researchers trying to replicate addiction in the laboratory. They tried inducing the "big four" of the addiction biases: craving, tolerance, dependence, and withdrawal. James Olds and Peter Milner, both psychologists, explained "addiction disease" by pointing to the conduct of rats in cages when subjected to the relentless stimulation of their brains' "pleasure centers" (the septal area of the hypothalamus).[20] The caged rats shot electricity to their brains as often as they could. This "reward model" of addiction helped substantiate the view of addiction as biomedical disease caused by the stimulation of "pleasure centers."

As a young student learning about Olds and Milner's rat research, I thought that there was little else for the rats to do in those terrible cages than to get high on electrical joy juice. The experiment did not explain human addictions. Drugs such as cocaine and heroin do produce extraordinary highs and they are profoundly addictive for some people; yet tobacco is just as addictive as these drugs, but it doesn't produce the equivalent highs.[21] The reward model also fails to explain why drug abuse continues even when unrewarding side effects such as anxiety, agitation, convulsions, and vomiting occur.

The biggest problem with the "reward model" of addiction is that it has been accepted by self-helpism as fact. In this uncomplicated view of the theory, something within us is subject to addiction, or is too weak to resist it. But remember Stanley Milgram's studies described in Chapter 1; they showed that it wasn't what was *inside* a person that made him or her willing to torture others, but something in the *situation* that encouraged bad conduct. The "within" belief bias of self-help often ignores the "between," or situational, factors involved.

In the early 1980s, creative and careful research by Bruce Alexander and his colleagues Roger Coambs and Patricia Hadaway challenged established thinking about addiction. They suggested that a broader view of the reward model can open new ways of dealing with the misery of real addiction and allow us to banish the myths that surround it.

A LESSON FROM RATS IN PARADISE

When Alexander observed laboratories where so-called "reward model" studies of addiction disease were taking place, he felt as I did. He saw skinny, starving, junkie rats with catheters sticking out of their heads living in feces-littered, cramped cages; every hour of their deprived existence was spent pushing levers that administered stimulation. He commented, "If I lived like that in a cage, I'd get as high as possible too."[22] He wondered whether testing animals in more benevolent settings would lead to the same kind of behavior shown by the addicted caged rats.

To test this hypothesis, Alexander and his research team built what they called a "rat park," or a rat paradise. They constructed a 200-square-foot rat housing colony, about the size of a small bedroom. It had heating, tasty cedar shavings, and the most preferred toys that could have come from "rats-R-us." The housing was co-ed with plenty of space for sex; the walls were hung with beautiful paintings that were the team's best guess as to what would make for rat heaven. A control rat group lived in the typical slums of laboratory cages.

The team then tempted the rat park and rat slum residents with morphine-laced water. The caged slum rats drank it until they fell into a drug-induced daze. The rat-parkers resisted the morphine water no matter how much sweetness was added to entice them. Some of the rat park residents would occasionally take a sip of the morphine water, but then returned to plain water. Living in rat paradise rendered the tempting joy juice nonaddicting. Even the rat-parkers who did imbibe to excess on the sweet morphine water eventually stopped drinking it. They did not "go into the throws of withdrawal" you might have seen portrayed in the movies; they just "came down," got up, and went back to enjoying life in rat park.

Alexander took a behavioral-cultural view of addiction. His research shows that addiction isn't caused by an abused inner child, an addicted parent, lingering childhood guilt, negative thinking, low self-esteem, an addiction gene, or the power of external temptation. Addiction is environmental more than psychological; it is caused by a situation, not a vulnerable psyche. Repeated exposure to even the most addicting drugs does not usually lead to addiction. It's not the drug we put in ourselves that's the problem but the place in which we find ourselves that leads to addictive behavior. Addiction appears to be related to whether we feel we are living in a terrible cage or in a loving colony.

Alexander calls addiction a "life-style strategy," and because it's a voluntary behavior engaged in to modulate unpleasant conditions, it's open to our own alteration. Although it may sound like heresy to all the AA twelve-step converts and other self-help programs for dealing with the multitude of alleged addictions, addiction is a life choice.

SELF-HELP HERESY

The victim mentality and "within" rather than "between" orientation permeates self-helpism. The religious approach of confessing your addiction and deferring to a higher power (God, a therapist, the group, the program) for helping you climb through steps to a life in perpetual recovery is the way of self-help. Although only about 5 percent of people in twelve-step programs succeed in staying sober, advocates still consider it heresy to challenge this approach.

The "cage vs. colony" idea is attacked by those who point out that wealthy people usually fill the luxurious beds at high-end addiction treatment centers. In both my clinical and personal experience, I have found that some of the richest people feel the most "caged in" and trapped in relationships, occupations, and lives characterized by great spiritual suffering. We've all heard stories about mega-millionaire rock stars and athletes who become addicted to drugs. On the other hand, many people struggling to make ends meet avoid drug use and addiction. Good relationships and membership in a caring colony make the difference.

I've also heard the argument that the brains of opioid, cocaine, and other drug abusers show signs of changes that weaken their ability to exercise free will. But as all scientists know, correlation is not causation. As with all the issues with which self-help deals, I suspect that there's a little truth in all the views of addiction. Creative self-help requires first being aware of these views and then carefully sorting through them to arrive at a dynamic view of the issue as it applies to one's own life.

MAYBE, MAYBE NOT

As we consider the mythology of self-helpism, it is helpful to consider a warning from President John F. Kennedy. He wrote, "The greatest enemy of truth is not the lie—deliberate, contrived, and dishonest, but the myth—persistent, persuasive, and unrealistic."

In Part II of this book, you will read about the creative self-help approach to seven major areas of life. I was concerned when the number turned out to be seven because so many self-help programs base their teaching on seven steps, or secrets. (Neuroscientists know that most people can easily hold seven items in memory, so it's no coincidence that phone numbers have seven digits, and Snow White had seven— not eight—dwarfs.)

The alternative ideas you will read about are suggestions, not instructions. By that, I mean the ideas are food for thought, not steps to take or concepts from which to begin a personal reconstruction program. I don't offer programs, steps, or answers; I do offer ideas that I hope you will find worthy of consideration for your own creative self-help program.

Self-helpism can't flourish unless we think something is wrong with us; the old psychology examined only those who were suffering and sick, leaving self-help free to encourage those who aren't "really sick" to become "all they can be."

Much of the new research that has relevance to what I'm calling creative self-help derives from the new field of positive psychology.[23] This is the science of what is right about us, and it goes beyond psychology's historical focus on what is broken and how to fix it to look instead at what is right and how to recognize it. The new positive psychology focuses on the ordinary magic of people who are thriving despite, and often because of, adversity. Joined by findings from the new fields of affective neuroscience, psychoneuroimmunology, energy cardiology, and other sciences generally unknown to the lay public, positive psychology offers a base for creative self-help.

Some Alternative "Facts of Life"

Here are some alternatives to self-helpism's "facts of life." They are meant to serve as catalysts for the more creative and contrarian consciousness and to provide direction for a more creative self-helping. I hope they will cause you to adopt a mindful approach to what is too often taken on faith.

Lose Hope.   Striving to keep your hopes up at the worst times in your life can be exhausting. Studies such as those recently conducted at the Harvard and UCLA Medical Schools show that hope does not promote healing, nor does it render cancer treatment more effective. Trying to "be hopeful" can prevent honest expression of feelings that could be helpful in maintaining and improving quality of life even at the most frightening times.

My own struggle with cancer taught me that pessimism, fear, anger, and panic are every bit as legitimate as constant hopefulness, and that such emotions are even essential. When others tell us not to lose hope, sometimes we hear, "Your present situation is terrible and all that's worth thinking about is a better future." Accepting that assessment is dangerously limiting because it tells us that the present is not all that worth living and that joy is to be found only in the future.

Give Up.   Persevering is not the only way to demonstrate strength. Nor is being strong always about working hard for victory over an outside obstacle. Strength can also mean knowing when to engage in enlightened surrender, willingness to give in and move on. Though giving up has a bad reputation in the self-help movement, winners do some-times intentionally quit, and quitters often end up winning.

Sometimes, persevering turns out to be glorious stupidity, and not giving up can lead to the loss of a golden opportunity. As the song says, the challenge is to "know when to hold them and know when to fold them." Too often we foreclose on today by constantly feeling pressured to struggle for a better tomorrow. So long as we give up both the striv-ing *and* the goal, we are free to think creatively about our problems. If, however, we just stop trying but still cling to our goal, we end up feel-ing despair and helplessness.

Think Sad Thoughts.   Trying to think only happy thoughts limits our ability to think creatively and critically. Our general level of happiness has almost nothing to do with external factors or how we "try to think"; it's largely due to our preset "happiness range"—from the annoyingly upbeat Winnie the Pooh to Eeyore the chronically down donkey. We are what we are and no amount of positive affirmation will change that. There's misery in the world and plenty to think sad thoughts about. Just as there is no day without night, we need sadness and sad thinkers as much as we need the gleefully upbeat. We all have our "happiness set point," one that is not changed by trying to think happier thoughts or by winning the lottery or "getting all the breaks."

Settle for Second (or Third or Sixth) Best.   In any life endeavor, there can be only one number one. Relax and enjoy being one of the thousands who fall short. My own research on successful people pub-lished in my book *Toxic Success* shows that misery is the ultimate result when we link our sense of achievement to other people's failures.

Don't "Work Through" Your Grief.   The pathogenic or "dysfunc-tional" starting point of most self-help approaches assumes that we need help with grieving and many other natural life transitions, that they are somehow "treatable." New research shows that there are many types of grieving and that the rush to grief counseling can do more harm than good by imposing assumptions that are not relevant to one's own grieving style.

Grieving is not a symptom. It is a natural, necessary life process. Because we live, we die. Because we die, we were made to grieve. As you read earlier, we are not emotional hydraulic machines in which our feelings build up a kind of spiritual steam that has to be vented. Unless we have other psychological problems, most of us grieve well without help, and do it relatively quickly without having to "work" at it or seek the help of a grief counselor.

Be a Pessimist. A little defensive pessimism goes a long way to building a good life. You'll seldom be disappointed, and sometimes pleasantly surprised. Unless you're a natural at trying to always think positively, the effort is stressful, exhausting, and limiting. A scientific *Journal of Negative Results* would likely contain many important lessons and new questions. Thinking negatively is easier and it comes naturally. If it didn't, our ancestors would not have survived. Our natural propensity for pessimism is a built-in evolutionary trait that helps keep us vigilant for threats to our well-being. Research indicates that the longest-living people in the world were distinguishable by their pessimistic outlooks.

Don't Try to Discover Your "Personal Power." You don't have nearly as much of it as you think, and you'll end up happier and healthier by focusing on your "interpersonal weaknesses."

Don't Believe in Yourself. No matter how much self-confidence you muster, you can't do *everything* you put your mind to. Part of the strength of giving up derives from avoiding the fatal mistake the legendary John Henry made: He tried to do the impossible. Beware of the "Little Engine That Could" approach to health. ("I feel O.K., I look O.K., I *am* O.K.!)

Don't Try to Have It All, Do It All, and "Just Say Yes."   It's exhausting and doesn't lead to nearly as much health and happiness as being willing to have less, do less, and just say no.

Stop Expressing, Representing, and Asserting Yourself.   Shut up and listen. Research shows that people who interrupt are three times more likely to die of a heart attack than those who don't and that marital relationships usually fail because of too much communication, not too little. Couples who spend a lot of time being quiet together stay together.

Men Aren't from Mars and Women Aren't from Venus.   One of my gay patients showed me relationship guru John Gray's book about the different planets from which men and women are supposed to come. He tossed it onto the table and said, "O.K., if this guy's right, on what planet do the gays, lesbians, and transsexuals live?" The problem isn't that men and women think as if they were from different planets; it's that they are following the wrong advice about how to live together on this one. Men and women are not nearly as different as we've been led to believe. (I have found that almost every major relationship book was written by a divorced author who had experienced many failed relationships.)

The oft-cited gender differences in these books are usually the reverse of what sound science says. It's men, not women, who tend to become emotional quickly, who tend to be clingy and needy, and who use an excess of words to express themselves. (One of my female patients said, "I know my husband uses a lot more words than I do. He just uses them all up before he gets home from work.")

You're Not a Victim.   Except for people who have suffered accidents and been victims of violent crime, most people are not victims of anything except thinking they're victims. Listen to any group of people talking about daily problems and you will hear the victim mentality, even if they are victims of something as inchoate as "the world today."

While we're examining self-help's victimology orientation, it's worth noting that most children aren't physically or emotionally abused. Those who were abused are not automatically doomed to lives of failure, to further victimization, or to victimizing others. Self-help psychology puts way too much emphasis on psycho-history, ignores the data showing that childhood experience doesn't have much to do with how people feel or act as adults, and neglects the strong influence of temperament.

Be a Good Blamer.   To err may be human, but to forgive is not always divine. There is a forgotten first step in the "forgive and move on" self-help advice—good, intense, mindful blaming. Finding the right person to blame is essential for good mental health.

Don't Read Weight-Loss Books: Eat Them.   They're a better source of fiber than information on permanent weight loss. If you eat them, they'll stay with you longer and be generally better for your bowels than the plans they offer.

Ditch Your Diet.   Research shows that no diet works for long, and constantly trying and failing at dieting is depressing, unhealthy, and ends up making you even fatter. Use the SWELMM system of "Stop Worrying, Eat Less, Move More."

Indulge Yourself.   Research on aging shows that the stamina and general good health shown by living long entitles older people to at least one pure indulgence a day for every ten years they have already lived. Whatever you've been doing is working, so reward yourself, and—despite Wayne Dyer's dire warnings about guilt—go ahead, feel guilty, and wallow in self-recrimination!

Bottle Up Your Anger.   Contrary to the idea that "letting it all out" is healthy, research by the physician Redford Williams and others shows that venting is bad for you and those around you. Do you remember your last intense angry rant? Did you feel better while you were doing it and after it? Did your tantrum target change? Research shows that although mindfully understanding your anger can be helpful, hostile expression of it weakens your immune system and literally hardens your heart and the hearts of those around you.

Show Your Age.   Gravity will trump nips, tucks, and Botox. No matter what you do, you will eventually grow old and wrinkled. Enjoy the fact that being old means you don't have to worry about dying young.

Don't Nurture Your "Inner Child"—Kick Its Ass.   Our well-being depends more on finding our "inner elder" than on yielding to a mythical, whining, narcissistic inner infant. Look for your problems within your adult interactions, not within your own infantilized consciousness.

Avoid Most Support Groups.   Talking with others about a real problem you share with them can be helpful, but many support groups often found that meeting at churches often became pseudo group therapy that, intentionally or not, ended up explaining and supporting destructive behavior rather than helping participants take individual responsibility for making the difficult long-term changes required. Gathering a bunch of self-proclaimed bulimics, shoplifters, and sexaholics together to discuss their afflictions can lead to group support "for" the problem rather than a careful examination of its roots.

Stop Mistaking Psychology for Religion.   Satan is not a personality disorder. It may be wise to learn from ancient spiritual systems and their forms of psychology and science, but modern psychology itself is—or should be—primarily a science, not a spiritual system. If you're looking for religion, get out of the self-help section of the bookstore and go to church or temple.

Face It, Your Family's Nuts.   The only cure for dysfunctional families is to do away with all families. We all have at least one weird family member and usually more. In fact, most of us *are* that member! A family is nothing more than a group of people irrationally committed to one another's welfare. Being a good family member means being able to enjoy living every day with a group of flakes and failures. A good family is a group willing to stick with you when most sane and discerning people would vote you out.

Deny Your Addiction.   Except for what seems to be a kind of "craze addiction" of "psychoholism" shown by dependence on the latest movement or program, most of us aren't and never will be addicted to anything. You're not a "chocoholic," you're just intentionally pigging out on chocolate because it tastes good. You're not a "sexaholic," you're just having too much reckless sex because it feels good. Even if one of our parents was a medically diagnosable alcoholic, long-term research shows that we are not doomed to suffer the same fate.

There are more stages to life than living in denial or recovery. Living in a state of assumed lifelong recovery wastes an enormous amount of creative energy. As I pointed out earlier, the famous twelve-step program is ineffective for 95 percent of those who attend it. The best way to deal with something you're doing that you shouldn't be doing is the one-step program: Stop it! A dose of good guilt and deserved shame might help.

Stop Looking for Mr. and Ms. Right.   Loving for life is not a matter of finding the right "someone." It's a matter of being the right person. No one is ever loved the way he or she wants to be loved. Stop looking for love and start showing it. Be more concerned with being love-worthy than being loved. Realize that it is at least as important to be in love with marriage as it is to try to find someone you would love to marry.

If You Think You've Fallen in Love, Get Up.   Psychologist Robert Sternberg shows that romantic love is a temporary mental "illness" or condition caused primarily by a state of neurohormonal imbalance. It is evolution's way of seeing that we propagate, but it doesn't cause us to cohabitate for long. If we calm down and wait, romantic love always passes and true love can grow.

Real love is not a feeling; it's a decision. If you think you're seeing love by gazing deeply into your partner's eyes, you aren't. You're seeing eyeballs. Lasting love is more a matter of learning to look outward at the world together than looking longingly eye-to-eye.

Love Conditionally.   Healthy, lasting love is conditional, not unconditional. No one, including you, is love-worthy if she or he does not behave lovingly. Love is something you earn, not something you deserve. Worry more about being love-worthy than about your own self-worth.

Delude Yourself.   Because we're all flawed and not easy to live with, every married person is married to a fool. Research shows that deluding oneself about one's partner—believing that he or she is kinder and more caring and helpful than he or she really is—is essential for a lasting relationship. The greater the discrepancy between close friends' more objective view of your marital partner and your own more subjective one, the happier and longer lasting the marriage.

Don't Expect What Goes Around to Come Around.   Total jerks and evil people often get all the good breaks. Being nice guarantees nothing. Good things happen to bad people. Sometimes, things just don't "balance out" or "work out for the best."

Stop Trying to Live Up to Your "Full Potential."   You probably don't have much more potential than you're showing right now, and striving for more will only cause disappointment. Stop focusing on your potential and start thinking about doing the best with the talents you already have.

Stop Trying to Correct Your Faults.   Instead, find your strengths and enhance those. Your biologically determined temperament accounts for a large percentage of your feelings and behavior. Striving to be someone you aren't leads to disappointment and, again, maybe even a heart attack. Despite all the self-help books, people don't ever really change all that much. The best we can do is to fine-tune our inherited temperaments.

Don't Strive to "Be All You Can Be."   Despite the exhortations of the recruitment ads for the United States military, that's a recipe for burnout. Keep a little in reserve. If you're all you can be, that's all you'll ever be. Trying to "be all we can be" assumes that we aren't all we can be right now, but we usually are.

Stop Trying to Retrieve Your "Repressed Memories."   Like many aspects of Sigmund Freud's theories that still permeate self-help (denial, defensiveness, passive-aggressiveness, etc.), research shows that the idea of repression, a mainstay of self-helpism, is out-of-date. As the psychologist Drew Westen pointed out: "Many aspects of Freudian theory are indeed out-of-date, and they should be. Freud died in 1939 and he has been slow to undertake further revisions."[24]

By considering these alternative facts of life and reflecting about them as they apply to your own life, you can begin the process of creative self-helping. By taking a "yes, but" mental attitude and reflecting on the opposite of the accepted tenets of the self-potential movement, you can discover new ways to find the meaning, comprehensibility, and manageability that truly allow you to help yourself. Through this more enlightened and inclusive self-helping, we help those who love us—and the world—and this is the path to fulfilling our true human potential.

Savoring Your Own Good Life

Our mindlessness regarding evaluation is perhaps
the greatest cause of our unhappiness.

ELLEN LANGER

I N THE INTRODUCTION to this book, I wrote about the concept
of *savoring* our lives. The desire to savor life is, I believe, what drives
many of us to the self-help aisle in the first place. Most of us are not
suffering a real addiction, not crippled by low-self esteem, not battling
repressed memories: These are the red herrings of the self-help movement. What really drives us to seek help is an equally frightening sensation: that of being alive, yet not really living.

THE SILENT EPIDEMIC

It is human nature to view the world, and to evaluate one's own life,
from one perspective. This doesn't allow for much relief from boredom
or anxiety, nor for much excitement even during the placidly "good"

times. We come to assess our lives as unchanging, static, less than they should be. As a result, we end up judging rather than savoring life.

This kind of mindless thinking has resulted in what research indicates is a silent but debilitating epidemic. It costs nearly $50 billion a year in absenteeism, diminished productivity, and treatment, and it affects almost eight out of ten people—but the toll on the human psyche is the most devastating aspect.[1] The condition leads millions to look for ways out of it: They search the self-help shelves in the bookstores, go to self-help retreats, and faithfully view teletherapy talk shows.

This epidemic of chronic daily discontent, or languishing, is defined as not feeling down, but not feeling up. In a sense, we're "losing all our marvels," and failing to relish our gift of being alive. Sufferers haven't lost their minds, just neglected them.

It is no surprise that this malaise has driven many of us to gurus who claim they have discovered the secret of savoring. But languishing may be caused by the idea that no matter how we are feeling, we owe it to ourselves to feel better. The unrelenting emphasis on self-improvement, on feeling better than well, on "being all you can be," has the opposite effect on most people. It makes us dissatisfied with ourselves and our lives.

MINDFULNESS VERSUS EVALUATION

But there is another way of confronting the languishing life. To savor life, to feel as though we experience every moment of it, good and bad, and are not passively watching it go by, we must learn to be mindful. Our use of evaluation, be it positive or negative, is at the root of our failure to enjoy life. Judging and comparing our lives rather than being fully engaged in everything—both good and bad—is the chief obstacle to the happiness of being alive.

Much of what I have written up to now is in the spirit of "mindfulness." The careful, deliberate thinking required to analyze the claims of self-help is a form of mindfulness. And finding positive ways to apply the suggestions of self-help to our own lives also requires that we be mindful. Psychologists who have studied the concept of mindfulness define it as claiming control of our consciousness by being vigilant about what we allow to enter it.

Psychologist Ellen Langer was the first to introduce mindfulness into modern psychology. She defined the concept as a flexible, contemplative state of mind achieved by taking charge of our own attention and not allowing it to be taken from us by the loudest, most visible, and most absolute declarative assertions. Mindfulness is much more than a mental trick: It's a way of engaging with the world. It's doing the hard work of establishing and maintaining control of our own attention in a world that constantly competes to rob us of it. It's "could and might be" and "yes, but" and contrary thinking rather than deference to someone else's certainty.

Mindfulness means always allowing ourselves "mental wiggle room," no matter how powerfully someone presents an idea to us. It means that we determine our quality of life by keeping control of what we have in our minds, not by practicing the latest program in which our thinking is done for us or embracing the biased beliefs that have become the McMorals of self-helpism.

Langer pointed out that mindfulness is being open to new and opposing ideas that at first glance may sound strange or even absurd.[2] Mindfulness is foregoing simple evaluation for deeper reflection: It's avoiding foreclosure on the future and giving up the past because of premature acceptance of what are presented to us as established "facts of life" in the present or promises for a better future.

To the impatient brain, mindfulness feels like "fuzzy thinking"—or analysis paralysis—that is never quite sure of anything. Mindfulness can be mistaken for mental sluggishness; to the busy brain it looks like mental flip-flopping because it involves looking for opposites and playing with ideas instead of blithely accepting them. Mindfulness is using the lessons of the past to bear on present ideas so that we will understand the future implications of these concepts. Mindfulness means not only being comfortable with uncertainty but seeking it, particularly when others are certain about something. And, finally, mindfulness means mentally just sitting there even when one is being pressured not to just sit there but to do something.

Langer points out that when we are mindful, we are guided by rules and routine; but when we are mindless, we allow ourselves to be governed by them. Creative self-help involves scientific thinking: learning what is known and then asking questions about it, forming hypotheses and testing them, sharing ideas with others who think scientifically, and always being open to learning. Compliant self-help accepts the ideas of someone else and puts them into practice before putting them to the test.

WHY POSITIVE THINKING IS DEPRESSING

An example of the mindless evaluative nature of self-help is its emphasis on "positive thinking" and on "repeating positive affirmations" to "drive them into" the unconscious mind. Research shows that depression relates to perfectionistic thinking, extreme and rapid emotional overreaction, taking things personally, and seeing events as pervasive and permanent. Mindfully reflecting about these findings led me to the conclusion that "thinking positively" can be depressing.

Affirmations such as "Every day in every way, I'm getting better and better" often contain the words "I" and "me" (personal), "everything" and "completely" (pervasive), and "always" and "from now on" (permanent). Such words are emotionally extreme and evaluative of the present situation instead of fully mindful of it.

THE WISDOM OF A FOUR-YEAR-OLD MIND

One example of mindful willpower is the classic "marshmallow study" in which four-year-old children learned to resist the immediate temptation of marshmallows and pretzels left in front of them.[3] The children were promised that they might be given more treats if they would not immediately devour the ones they saw.

The children in one group were taught to resist the temptation of the treats through a more mindful approach to the situation. They were shown how to "re-frame" (re-mind) the immediate temptation and quick evaluation of the situation by mentally cooling down and taking the time to consider and reflect on their present circumstances in a fuller and richer context. They were told to think of the marshmallows as puffy clouds rather than chewy sweets, and the pretzels as tiny logs rather than crunchy treats.

The children in the "mindful" group were shown how to use their minds instead of following the urgings of hurried and hungry brains. Because they were taught how to "cool down" the stimulus, these children found the will and wisdom to wait almost three times longer than the more mindless "hot and go" control group of children, who were left to react immediately to the seductive power of the moment.

When the mindfulness-tutored children finally ate the marshmallows and pretzels as well as the extra reward they received for their waiting, they benefited twice. They had savored the moment by waiting amidst images of clouds and logs and had relished the anticipation of the extra tasty treats that would reward their reflective patience. We might imagine, as well, that the treats were sweeter for the wait.

HAPPINESS STRESS

The poet Yevgeny Yevtushenko calls our attention to "the vulgar, insultingly patronizing fairy tale that has been hammered into our heads since childhood that the main meaning of life is to be happy."[4] To self-helpism, "happy" is the equivalent of high self-esteem, and when we embrace only this approach to "the" good life, we end up like self-absorbed adolescents interested only in how we feel.

Savoring our lives is a mindful alternative. Psychologists Fred B. Bryant and Joseph Veroff of Loyola University define savoring as the awareness of deliberate, conscious attention to the things, persons, and events that bring us pleasure.[5] Based on the research on mindfulness, I would replace "that bring us pleasure" with "that make us feel fully alive."

Bryant and Veroff identify four kinds of savoring, including basking (enjoying things that make us feel good), thanksgiving (expressing gratitude for blessings), marveling (losing the self in the wonder of the moment), and luxuriating (indulging the senses). Each of these implies enjoying something good that enhances our experience of life, and no one can argue with their importance for well-being. But what about their opposites? Are there any mental, emotional, spiritual, or even physical lessons to be learned from moping, griping, boredom, and self-denial? I'm not sure, but I've found that mindful thinking about the other side of savoring helps me come up with new and interesting perspectives on life. I have found that some of my darkest moments are also the times when I'm the most creative.

DARK CLOUDS WITH GRAY LININGS

The more mindful about hope I became when I was ill, the more I realized that having hope was often easier than giving it up and becoming fully engaged in the lessons of my suffering in the present moment. As I learned about the depressing nature of positive thinking, I came to think that I needed my despair and my current fear as much as my anticipation of a better tomorrow. I decided to try giving up hope again, but more mindfully this time. The self-help books about hope had helped, but only because of a mindful reflection about their ideas.

I remember that late one night a nurse was trying to cheer me up. I was crying and deeply contemplative about the meaning of the loss I predicted for myself and my family. There was something sacred and powerfully instructive about those down moments, but this particular nurse was a dyed-in-the-wool self-help fan. She said, "I just read a book about miracles in medicine and how hope heals and how you can think yourself well. It's mind over matter. Never lose hope. Remember, every dark cloud has a silver lining. Tomorrow is another day."

As the smiling nurse left the room, I felt as if I had just had my today taken from me. The nurse was telling me that I was failing by not being hopeful and thinking optimistically about the future and that there was little worth thinking about in this present moment of my suffering. This theory mistook healing for not feeling sick and never feeling sad for long. The nurse was saying that my current state had no value and that I should spend my time thinking that I must and would get past this bad moment as soon as possible and start immediately hoping for something better tomorrow.

The nurse's mention of dark clouds "re-minded" me that I had always loved dark clouds. They were filled with possibilities, full of vital energy yet to be expressed. Their darkness gave them a much different kind of potential than that of fluffy white clouds. I had always noticed that the darker the cloud, the more pensive I was and the more depth and range I brought to my feelings and thinking.

I needed my gray and dark times perhaps in different ways, but I needed them just as much as I needed rays of hope. The issue was "and," not "or." There was something energizing and uplifting about hope for the future, but there was also something magnificently vibrant and life-affirming about the dark times of my despair. Even in pain, I needed to be as fully alive and conscious as possible.

I spent months in agonizing pain. Chemotherapy, full-body radiation, and a bone marrow transplant had left me so weak that I could barely lift my arms. At first I thought that hope was all I had and that joy in life had to lie somewhere in the future. But hours of reflection led me to believe that this illness-imposed time of passivity, dependence, and immobility was also affording me the opportunity to focus on memories, the love I had for my family, the first light of day, the sound of rain on the cement sill outside my window and the origins and destination of that rain, and the meaning of life and death.

Something about the badness of illness and the fear of death brought out the goodness of living, and the more my body failed me, the more I found my mind. The less I evaluated my situation positively and the more I mindfully lived it, the more I saw that too much time spent hoping was taking me away from being. I began to seek a balance between looking forward to a better day and freeing myself from negatively evaluating today.

TRANS-PARENT SURGERY

We shrink from accepting the bad with the good out of a fear that the bad will contaminate the good. This is reinforced by the self-help notion of damaged psyches: The wounded soul needs help to heal, we're told, or it will remain forever crippled. But in my own life and in my practice, I have seen ample evidence that this is simply not true.

In 1979, a psychiatrist from New York called me at my clinic to consult me about what he called "a really weird situation." He had begun to treat a family he said he would never forget; indeed, his experience had caused him to abandon much of his psychoanalytic orientation and ideas about the vulnerability of the developing childhood psyche. I arranged with my colleague to follow the progress of each of the four children in the years to come.

I had never heard of a more catastrophic family environment. The father and mother had been repeatedly arrested for selling and using drugs. The father had become a member of "sexaholics anonymous," a self-help twelve-step treatment program offered by a "commitment coach" and self-proclaimed sex therapist, but his conduct did not change. He said he often lost his temper and used his belt to spank his children for the most minor offenses, and particularly when they got in the way of his "sex parties." These parties were orgies that he called his "Spaghetti and Meat Ball Bashes," his code for Sadism and Masochism. The orgies took place only a few feet from the bedrooms where his children slept.

The mother in this poster marriage for pathology was severely depressed. By her own report, she had become a "sex pawn" in her husband's orgies. After several years of what would appear to guarantee severely damaged children, things became even more bizarre. After years of therapy with the New York psychiatrist and four attempts at sex addiction therapy programs, the parents thought they had finally identified their problems: They were trapped in the wrong bodies. They each had sex change surgery and underwent hormonal therapy to change their genders. Over the next two years, the father became the children's mother and the mother became their father.

When I spoke to the four now-grown men and women who had spent their childhoods in this family circus of sick behaviors, I expected to hear about serious problems. Certainly there would be addiction, sexual problems, divorce, and other struggles for all of them. I was wrong. All four adults had married, were still married when I spoke with them, and were still the same gender. I spoke with each of their spouses, who reported no unusual problems (or parties). All the grown children now had several children of their own who were doing just fine. All four reported gratifying sexual relations in their marriages, verified by their spouses. All had graduated from college, two had earned postgraduate degrees, and one was a physician. None reported substance abuse or addiction and none had been in therapy. They all said their lives were what one of them described as "boringly normal."

Here is the perfect example of how light can overcome life's darkness. No doubt these four people wished their childhoods had been different (many of us do). And I do not suggest that their early trials made them happy adults. I tell their story to disprove the superstition that bars many of us from mindfully embracing all of life: that by accepting dark days, we forfeit the good ones.

Of course, one remarkable case does not prove my point about the felicity of self-help's beliefs, and it's not intended to. No one would wish on any child the experiences these four people endured; but years of research on child development show that what happens to us as kids is not nearly as important as we have been told it is.[6]

DR. BUDDHA'S FOUR TRUTHS

Mindfulness as a concept originated 2,500 years ago; its roots are found in Buddhist teachings, and particularly in the third of Buddhism's Four Noble Truths. (If Buddha were alive today and willing to offer his teachings through modern marketing, he might well be called "Dr. Buddha," his books would top the best-seller lists, he would offer retreats and seminars, and he would be in demand as a motivational lecturer by Fortune 500 companies.)

> The First Truth is that suffering is subjective, natural, necessary, and is part of the gift of life. We would help ourselves more if we remembered that lesson and did not ask of life what it cannot give us: unrelenting total contentment and happiness. Despite the claim that we can "have it all," we can't; we can end up killing ourselves and ruining our relationships by trying. We're made to feel guilty and happy, sad and gleeful, and to be down as much as up.

That's the gift of being a dynamic and developing person. Living in a static and predictable state might sound appealing, but if you mindfully reflect on such boring sameness, you'll come to think of it as a curse.

The Second Truth is that our suffering is made worse because we think we shouldn't *have* to suffer. We react to this spiritual sissy-hood by coveting and becoming attached to things and ideas that we think will reduce our suffering. A fixation on high self-esteem often becomes that kind of attachment.

The Fourth Truth. (No, I didn't forget number three. It's next, and out of what has become the linear pop psychology step-by-step order.) This truth teaches that we are able to regain control of our minds. We can free ourselves from the "monkey minded-ness" of automatically reacting to the most immediate stimuli and from seeking the easiest and quickest way of acquiring what we think we want or are told we want. Self-help programs promise quick and immediate relief from whatever ails us; but creative self-help involves questioning whether we really are "ail-ing" and, if we are, contemplating whether it is best to keep moving to a quick state of relief that makes us forego today for the promise of a better tomorrow.

The Third Truth. The preceding three Truths relate to mindfulness, but the Third Truth most clearly defines it. This truth teaches that the peace of mind and contented heart we so desperately seek do not depend upon external circumstances, other persons' ideas or programs, constantly feeling happy, never feeling guilty, or any one thing or idea. Peace of mind is not an achieved state of high self-esteem or the final break from the bond of child-hood past. The Third Truth is a way of thinking and developing that incorporates full conscious awareness and contemplation of one's present life and the full range of emotions that awareness generates.

Psychologists who have studied the concept of mindfulness define it as claiming control of the content of our consciousness by being vigilant about what we allow to enter it. Put simply, it's contemplation, not evaluation; it's slow and long thinking rather than the fast and short acceptance of someone else's thinking. Mindfulness is restraining our runaway brain by taking time to calm down and think for ourselves, but not just *about* ourselves. Mindfulness is how we learn to savor life and as such is the key to creative self-help.

RE-MINDING OURSELVES

Here's a summary of the nature of mindfulness as described by Langer and others. I suggest you put your mind to the following ideas about a more creative consciousness as paths for savoring your life now.

- Remain aware that it's mindfulness, not positive evaluation, that leads to a life well savored.
- Question the underlying values and premises not only of others but on which your own evaluations are built.
- Think about the conditions under which you might change your mind instead of offering defending hypotheses to keep it closed.
- Seek wisdom and enlightenment from within and with others and not just in reaction to attention-demanding stimuli.
- Consider the past and future as well as the present, but do not become bound in any one of those times.
- Be subjective toward others as people while remaining objective about their ideas and recommendations.
- Be a "hard sell" when it comes to "how to do it" by thinking slowly, deeply, and paradoxically; give yourself the mental time to develop your own mindful wisdom so that you will no longer need to defer to the most popular, strongly promoted, and authoritatively presented ideas.

- Value being confused and being left with more questions than answers.
- Most of all, find the light within by thinking for yourself without thinking only about yourself.

THE WISDOM OF BEING "LIGHT"-HEADED

The life of the French author Jacques Lusseyran, one of my colleagues at the University of Hawaii, offers an example of the kind of savoring mindfulness that can lead to the "light" described above.

Totally blind since the age of eight, Lusseyran graduated from college, printed an underground newspaper when he was in the French Resistance during World War II and despite being tortured and starved in a concentration camp, he became an inspiration to the other prisoners there. He managed to find food for the sickest prisoners and helped build a secret radio receiver right under the noses of the guards. He had been captured because an informant had infiltrated the newspaper staff. Lusseyran had doubted the man was the right person to join the resistance movement, but everyone else at the paper had been convinced by the man's presentation. Lusseyran went along.

Referring in part to the regret he felt for not following his own sense about his betrayer and for not resisting the popular consensus, he described his sense of mindfulness. He wrote: "Whatever happens to us, it is within. The light does not come to us from without. Light is in us, even if we have no eyes."[7]

Savoring our own good life requires giving up the search for the one good life and mindfully examining the prescriptions for it. Consider the words of E. L. Doctorow: "When ideas go unexamined and unchallenged for a long time, certain things happen. They become mythological, and they become very, very powerful." Part II of this book invites you to challenge that power.

. . . And How It Can

In order to arrive at what you are not,
You must go through the way
In which you are not.

T.S. ELIOT, *THE FOUR QUARTETS*

4

Developing a Contrarian Consciousness

Without contraries, there is no progression.

WILLIAM BLAKE

I F YOU TORE a page from this book and folded it in half, then in half again, and continued to do this a hundred times, how thick does your intuition tell you your creation would be? An inch, a foot, maybe even a yard? The answer is eight hundred *trillion* times the distance between the Earth and the sun![1] Most people are shocked by this fact because it runs counter to what their intuition tells them, and that's one of the problems with the assertions of self-helpism. They just make intuitive sense—they "sound right." That doesn't mean they are.

Most of us sense an innate validity to the basic self-help concepts. Their appeal is that they feel right, they make us feel good at least for a while, and like fast food, we can take them in quickly and easily. But they are really a set of McMorals, tenets about life that go down easily but aren't good for our long-term well-being. They don't always hold up to mindful thought that looks at them from a scientific point of view.

I'm not suggesting that our intuition is always wrong, only that we can't always trust it to be right. Self-help's premises and plans for "the good life" have persevered because we have failed to put them to the test. Creative self-help begins with feeling skeptical, not inspired. It requires the philosopher Paul Kurtz's view of a skeptic: "One who is willing to question any truth claim, asking for clarity in definition, consistency in logic, and adequacy of evidence."[2]

What's needed to overcome our reliance on intuition is a contrarian consciousness. Think of the typical "contrary child," refusing to go along, insisting that things be different. Although you might not want to sit next to such a child on an airplane, she can be a useful mental companion. When we apply a contrarian consciousness to an idea, we can find startling truths that we never would have seen otherwise. Going back to Galileo, one can easily find examples of men and women who were repeatedly told a "fact"—"the Earth is flat"—yet who stubbornly questioned, doubted, and contradicted until they were able to prove a new idea—"the Earth is round." Adopting this kind of outlook can have nearly as revolutionary an effect on our own lives as Galileo's did on the world.

HOT AND COLD RUNNING PEOPLE

Contrarian thinking, then, requires that we resist our natural instincts to follow the herd. It means using a "cooler and calmer" thinking style about emotionally "hot" self-help concepts that urges us to be quick thinkers always moving onward and upward, faster and faster.

By examining how people mentally deal with challenges in their lives, John Metcalfe and Walter Mischel, both cognitive psychologists, were the first to distinguish between and study "cool and know" (mindful) and "hot and go" (mindless) psychological systems.[3] Their research showed that the "hot and go" system is an intuitively reactive kind of thinking based on one of self-help's favorite philosophies, "If it feels good, do it." The "cool and know" reaction is more mindful, and more contrary. It employs the "if it feels good, first think about it" reaction. It is a process of slow looking and long thinking that evokes a rational and reflective mind.

We can't really be contrary without adopting the "cool and know system," and it may be the "hot and go" mindless way of dealing with the world that is often referred to as our "addictive tendencies." It's our hot-and-go system that can cause us to forget safe sex when we are under strong sensual temptation. The four-year-old children in the marshmallow study (discussed in Chapter 3) found that their thoughtfulness led them to delay action and make a wiser choice; we will find, as they did, that the mindful cool-and-know system can give us mental resources that provide the willpower and the time to become wiser in our choices.

THE POWER OF THE MADE-UP MIND

In 1979, the psychologist Charles Lord and his colleagues provided another classic study illustrating how difficult it is to change beliefs.[4] They studied people with opposing views on the controversial issue of capital punishment. They gave both groups two sets of research findings, one set that supported the claim that the death penalty deters crime and another set refuting that position. The subjects ended up being more impressed with the studies that supported their original beliefs, and all disputed the findings of the opposing studies. Thus, instead of leading to a more mindful consideration of the issue, the mix of studies on both sides showed that the pro- and anti-death-penalty groups strengthened their original convictions.

If we want to rein in the power of our belief biases, and our blind trust in our own intuition, we have to be aware of the psychological phenomenon of *belief perseverance*. Once we have decided that we believe something, we will tend to keep on believing it, even in the face of disconfirming evidence.

It can be embarrassing to climb down from our previous assertions. It is also difficult to remove a belief that has been woven into a wider web of belief without disturbing those other beliefs. This issue becomes increasingly important when viewed in a world where nationalistic and religious beliefs become the basis for intolerance and violence. (Listen to people talking during a political election and you will hear belief perseverance in full tilt.)

QUITE THE CONTRARY

But can the power of our belief perseverance be overcome by information that clearly discredits our biases? Not necessarily. A study by the psychologists Craig Anderson and Lee Ross showed just how difficult it is to change a belief once a person is given ideas that support it.[5] They asked a group of people to consider whether risk takers or cautious people make better firefighters. They told one half of the people a story about a risk taker whose quick action made him an excellent firefighter and another story about a cautious person whose hesitation made him a poor firefighter. From these manufactured cases, the subjects decided that risk takers make better firefighters. The researchers then gave the other half of the study group two cases suggesting the opposite conclusion; this group decided that cautious people think before they act and make fewer mistakes. Nothing much surprising about these findings, but that was not the most interesting part of Anderson and Ross's experiment.

When the researchers discredited the bases for the beliefs of both groups by telling them that the cases were fabricated, we might assume that the participants would abandon their falsely created beliefs. They did not. They held to them and continued to present the same explanations for them as they had done when they trusted the bogus stories.

We see this "sticking to our guns" mentality in all aspects of our lives from political campaigns to marital conflict; therefore, changing our beliefs about something as firmly established and trusted as self-help's assertions about daily living and loving is not an easy task, but that's the whole point. Real creative self-help, the kind that leads to substantive and lasting change, isn't easy. Just because beliefs are presented in simple terms that appear to be a perfect match for our hunches doesn't make them right.

Years later, Lord and his colleagues repeated their capital punishment study with other groups. This time, they asked one group to be "as objective and unbiased as possible" after considering their reading. The plea had no effect on the entrenched beliefs of either side as to the value of capital punishment. However, when they asked another group to think contrarily by asking "Would you have made the same high or low evaluations had exactly the same study produced results on the other side of the issue?" participants became much less biased in their evaluation of the evidence.[6] By persuading the groups to look at the data from a "contrary" perspective, progress was made in loosening the grip of the "belief perseverance effect."

Most self-help gurus hold firmly entrenched beliefs, and as the political scientist Robert Jarvis pointed out, "Once you have a belief, it influences how you perceive all other relevant information."[7] Sigmund Freud, whose emotional hydraulic belief still holds sway in self-help, wrote that his ideas had "gained such a hold" upon him that he could "no longer think in any other way." I even found the belief perseverance phenomenon scrawled in graffiti as an expression by a Ray Charles fan. It said, "God is love, love is blind, Ray Charles was blind, Ray Charles is God."

SOME IDEAS OF MINE
THAT YOU SHOULD NOT ACCEPT

The rest of this book presents new ways of looking at self-help's facts of life. They are the result of years of my own attempts to reflect mindfully about the ways to love, work, raise children, heal when hurt, and deal with adversity, grief, and mortality. My take on these ideas is based on my reading of the research related to self-help's recommendations and philosophies. I reconsider this research often, keeping an open mind and reconsidering "the facts."

My version of creative self-help propositions are more like propaedeutics. The word "propaeduetics" refers to ideas and concepts that are preparatory to the study of a particular field, and I offer mine only as starting points, not as the "ultimate keys" to a better life.

SHATTERING THE TEN COMMANDMENTS

To help you prepare for reflecting about my creative self-help propositions, I invite you to begin by considering my contrarian alternatives to each of self-help's commandments. I present them here alongside the original top ten hits, in language reflecting the zeal with which self-help's concepts are embraced.

TEN CONTRARY COMMANDMENTS OF SELF-HELP

Self-Help Commandment	*Contrary Consideration*
1. Thou shalt not love another person until thou love thyself.	*Thou shalt learn to love others in order to become love-worthy.*
2. Thou shalt never think negatively, feel guilty, or have a pessimistic attitude.	*Thou shalt seek lessons from insights from a gloomy attitude, negative thinking, inspiration for change from one's guilt, and authenticity through the mindful experience of all emotions.*
3. Thou shalt never give up hope.	*Thou shalt embrace feelings of hopelessness as a source of mental and spiritual relief from the stress of constant striving, a warning not to foreclose prematurely on today in favor of the unfilled promises of tomorrow, and a chance to glimpse meaning in pessimism and doubt.*

4. Thou shalt never be less than thou can be.	*Thou shalt celebrate what thou already art, look to build on thine strengths rather than correct thine weaknesses, not assume thine own happiness is the purpose of life, and appreciate what thou has.*
5. Thou shalt not be codependent.	*Thou shalt cherish the power of creative codependence, bask in the comforting grace of deference, and relish the soothing peace of compliance.*
6. Thou shalt not fail to set goals and achieve them.	*Thou shalt give up not only the goal but the effort, practice creative quitting, let go, give in, accept defeat, and not find thine own success in another's failure.*
7. Thou shalt get in touch with thine feelings and express them.	*Thou shalt be out of touch with thine own feelings and in touch with those of others.*
8. Thou shalt not love conditionally.	*Thou shalt love as one desires to be loved, and not forgive those who ask for love without giving it.*
9. Thou shalt not live in denial.	*Thou shalt savor the calmness afforded by enlightened denial and the peace of self-delusion.*
10. Thou shalt never hold anger in.	*Thou shalt contain thine anger, for expressed anger is the kindling for more anger and its heat consumes those who express it and those toward whom it is expressed.*

"Just Consider It"

I offer no prescriptions in the following chapters, only ideas to think about. The mindful, contrarian way of thinking about these ideas offers real self-help and shows that we have proceeded much too quickly to "how to do it" before spending nearly enough time in "how to think about it." And the more often you thoughtfully disagree with me, the more successful I will have been in challenging you to consider a more mindful perspective about what you have been told.

Here are some of the ideas that have grown out of my own contrarian view of self-help's assertions:

Don't buy a self-help book just because the author has a Ph.D. or M.D. Being educated in one area doesn't make someone an expert in all areas. And plenty of degree holders fail to think scientifically. (Only 30 percent of American Psychological Association members read that organization's own professional journals.[8])

Don't be impressed with celebrity. Lesser-known laypersons and professionals write some of the most helpful self-help books. Be a cautious and smart self-help shopper. A high fee for a motivational speech doesn't necessarily mean that it's worth it for you.

Don't buy a self-help book or series of books by only one author. Belief bias will prevent the author from giving you the "whole picture."

Apply the same standards to self-helpers, trainers, and motivationalists as you would to hiring someone to manage your finances.

Consider the purchase of a self-help book or training program much as you would the purchase of a car. Look around, think about, and talk to someone who owns it and has tried it out.

Don't forget that self-help is a business. Authors and publishers want you to buy, read, be convinced by what you read, and buy again. That doesn't mean their books don't have value, only that we should approach them as careful consumers making a purchase, not as patients hiring a virtual therapist.

Don't buy only one book on a particular subject. Marketing pressure dictates that self-help books address one specific problem, not all of life. Life doesn't work that way because all of our problems are interrelated.

Ignore the "blurbs" from celebrities and other authors. If they were right, every book would be "the definitive ground-breaking book" on whatever it is about. Many of the providers of testimonials for books know one another, provide testimonials as favors, and often don't read the book.

Flip immediately to the back pages of a self-help book. If there's no sign of a bibliography or reference section, put it back. It helps to know whether the author knows about other work in the area and how the author came to those conclusions. Self-help books aren't "peer reviewed" as professional journals are, so their authors can say anything they please.

Don't buy a self-help book because the author or the public relations material says it's a "best-seller." There's no law regulating the use of that word.

Be suspicious, be very suspicious, of books with numbers in the title. Numbering the keys to the good life may be good marketing, but life is not linear and solving its problems doesn't usually work according to numbers. Fifteen years and 15 million copies of his 7 *Habits of Highly Effective People* later, self-help guru Stephen Covey has added a number. He says he's discovered an "eighth habit" from "the third dimension."

Before you try to apply advice to your own life, don't just seek a second opinion from someone who has tried it. Self-help buyers can develop a fierce loyalty to their favorite experts and programs that can blind their objectivity. Ask someone who would never buy the book you have bought to read it and give his or her opinion about its value. Don't accept that opinion, but reflect on it mindfully before you start "on the program."

Buy a used introductory psychology textbook. Search the index for your problem, read the section or sections that are related to your concerns, write down the names of the researchers mentioned, and then look in the bibliography for the works the researchers have written. (I hope you will look at the reference section of this book.) Go to the library and read about their research and views.

Don't be seduced by "new" approaches to the "good life." Self-help dates back 3,500 years to ancient Egyptian and Greek writings. Modern approaches to self-helping are only the most recent attempts to ease troubled minds, so mindfully looking on your own past "new age" to "old age" wisdom in classic writings and teachings can offer some good food for thought.

Don't confuse psychotherapy, counseling, training, or coaching with "psychology." Most therapists are usually teaching their own life belief biases, not offering scientifically based concepts. Academic research-based psychology has traditionally been the primary source of challenges to the efficacy of these approaches and shows that most "therapy" advice from an "expert" is no more helpful than advice from a good friend.

Don't assume that therapists, counselors, trainers, and coaches know anything at all about psychology. They are usually offering their own take on general life principles and have no more idea about a good life than you do. Research shows that most of those who claim these titles don't use the classic and new psychology research studies in their work, and most don't even know about them.[9]

Peg the period. To be clear of its beginning belief bias, this means looking for the origins of the kind of thinking that is the basis of the advice being given. For example, "steam" thinking characterized the nineteenth century and resulted in the still-dominant "emotional hydraulic" bias ("let it all out"—"vent pent-up emotions"—"running out of steam"). "Electrical" thinking began in the early twentieth century, the result being a "stored energy" bias ("getting charged up"—"being energized"—"tapping into personal power"—"feeling fun down"). After World War II, "computer thinking" led to "data" bias ("memory storage"—"dumping"—"online"—"real time"—"deleting and crashing"—"logging on and off").

Information is not power. Information is just information until we use our mindful understanding to assess it and put it in meaningful and useful context. Sometimes, the more information you acquire, the more confused you become, resulting in "fact fatigue" from so many sure answers to everything.

Beware the "Barnum Effect." This is a well-researched psychological principle based on P. T. Barnum's famous statement, "There's a sucker born every minute." It is our documented gullibility to believe written descriptions of ourselves and our lives just because they're in writing, an expert wrote them, and—like horoscopes—they are so broadly written that they can't be too wrong or too right.

Read what satirists have to say about self-help. They can be cruel and they drastically distort the views of self-help and its gurus, but that's what gives satire its power to cause open minds to think in new ways about accepted ideas. It can help us hone our mindfulness by challenging self-help's sacred cows and offering a contrary view from someone who has absolutely no faith in them. When I was desperately ill, I found books like these books at least as helpful as the best-selling self-help books. A few of my current favorites are listed in the footnotes for this chapter.[10]

Don't stop buying self-help books. Just because they are biased doesn't mean there aren't some good ideas in them worth your mindful critical thinking.

I hope these suggestions will help you think in different ways about what everybody intuitively "knows" about a good life. There *is* one approach that is worth considering if you decide to examine your beliefs about the self-help movement's assertions and programs, and that's contrarian consciousness. As you read the following chapters, I hope you will look where I'm pointing and not bite my finger. As the philosopher Arthur Schopenhauer wrote, "The task is not so much to see what no one yet has seen, but to think what nobody yet has thought about that which everybody sees."

Love Lies and Why We Believe Them

To love, be lovable.

OVID

PROPOSITIONS ABOUT LOVE

1. You have to learn to love others before you can love yourself.
2. True love is not emotional; it's volitional.
3. Enduring love is conditional, not unconditional.
4. Healthy love is a matter of being the right partner, not finding the right person.
5. Lasting love is based on mutual delusion.

MISMANAGED UNIONS

Would you like to be in the top 10 percent of the happiest people in the world, enhance your own physical and mental health, and add an average of four years to the length of your children's lives? If so, consider entering into a close, mutually nurturing, tolerantly delusional, equitable, mutually dependent companionship with your best friend. For brevity's sake, I will call this relationship a marriage. I will refer to the force that bonds and maintains it the "L" factor, the designation used by the most careful scientific researchers for the mysterious bonding power of caring connection and selfless sharing.[1]

The health and happiness benefits of being married have been well-documented by a century's worth of research, and these studies show that married people are not just smarter, nicer, and happier people in the first place. Even when serious illness or other crises strike and make us unhappy and miserable to live with, marriage is still one of society's strongest predictors of happiness, healing, and hardiness.[2]

Psychologist David Myers called marriage "the union that defies management."[3] When I told a lecture audience that my wife, Celest, and I had been married for forty years, a man yelled incredulously, "To each other?" The only thing stable about the institution of marriage is its failure rate. In Canada and the United States today, one out of two marriages fails, and the effects are devastating.[4] We often hear that "marriage is the cornerstone of the family." The sacredness of male-female marriage as an institution is touted by those who oppose gay marriage and see it as a danger to the very fabric of our society, but that cloth is already pretty ragged. Indeed, the track record of heterosexual marriage is so dismal that one might wonder why any homosexual would want to consider such a union.

LESSONS FROM TERMITES

The Terman Life-Cycle Study was a revolutionary psychological study of gifted girls and boys, whom researchers referred to as "the Termites." When Howard Friedman, a psychologist at the University of California at Riverside, looked at the life spans of termites, he and his colleagues discovered something alarming: Divorce has lasting health effects on children.[5] The researchers found that children younger than twenty-one when their parents divorced had a 30 percent higher risk of early death than children from intact marriages; this means that adults whose parents were divorced die on average four years earlier than adults whose parents stayed married.

When Friedman looked at the marriages of the grown-up Termites, he found the same negative health effects of divorce. Divorced women were 80 percent more likely to die young than those who stayed married; and for divorced men, the chances of an early death were increased 120 percent! Serial marriages carried their own threat to longevity. For those Termites who inconsistently married, meaning those who divorced and remarried, the risk of early death was 40 percent higher than consistently married Termites.

WHY HAPPILY MARRIED PEOPLE AREN'T IN LOVE

Many people ask more of marriage than they are willing to contribute. We are asking our marriages to serve as romantic self-help programs through which we become whole by finding our "other halves." We would do well to learn from the research on marriage that love is a verb, not a noun.

Long-married people aren't *"in* love" with each other, at least not in the sense of tingling romanticism. Although they certainly have positive feelings for each other, they "love" each other through diligent delusion regarding each other's faults and frailties. They are in love with marriage: For long-married people, marital improvement is more important than self-improvement. They have learned that we have more chance of finding the happiness and health we so desperately seek if we put more effort into helping the marriage than in helping the "self."

Research shows that staying married is one of the most important things we can do if we want to live long and well, but in spite of the hundreds of books about how to find the right lover, how to date by the right rules, and how to rescue troubled relationships, many us haven't yet mastered the art of *lasting* love.

Why is it that we are so bad at doing something we sense is so good and that research shows is good for us? Are we raising our children to be so focused on having lives that are better than ours that we fail to show that we regard, honor, and nurture marriage as the core of the family? I suggest that such failure is self-help's legacy of lost love.

As you will read in Chapter 6, research shows that although we do not abuse, neglect, or exploit our children nearly as much as the child-history bias and the repressed memory belief bias suggest, we do cause them to suffer from "dyadal deprivation," the most predictive factor for staying physically healthy and living a long life. Dyadal deprivation means the failure to grow up in a house with two adults—whom teenagers now revealingly call "parental units"—who regularly show their love for each other and keep showing it for a lifetime.

WHY CAN'T WE STAY TOGETHER?

Why are we so good at falling in love and so bad at staying in it? Why do we so often make liars of ourselves by pledging love until death and then failing to maintain it? Is our vow to love forever really only a wish to continue feeling turned on? Why do we struggle so to stay in love when it is so easy to fall into in the first place? With all the self-help advice available to us from the relationship experts, why can't we get love right and make it last? Is the solution to be much more cautious about the whole idea and, as many self-help guides suggest, "test the marital waters" first by living together before sealing the deal? Does trying out a relationship through a practice marriage lead to a more stable marriage later? Again, classic studies from psychology don't provide "answers," but they do suggest that the self-help approach isn't the best way to learn how to capture the "L" factor within a relationship.

It's no wonder we can't tickle ourselves. We're prewired to need others to stimulate our senses, but despite the hundreds of love manuals advising us about how we can learn to love ourselves as a prerequisite to loving someone else, our relationships are still failing at high rates. No matter how many relationship guides we purchase, the Beatles song "Can't Buy Me Love" still rings true.

Self-help's emphasis on self-esteem may have contributed to many of the problems in learning how to love for life. Instead of looking for someone with whom we *think* we could create a good life, we search for an idealized person who makes us feel good, but the "feeling good" usually turns out to be temporary.

There's a lot of talk about falling in love with one's "soul mate." We unwittingly lie about "feeling like this forever" and possessing "never-ending love." But we talk less about what it really takes to remain in love with one partner for a lifetime. The French have a saying: "Love makes the time pass and time makes love pass." But does it have to be that way?

Premarital Testing

As one approach to thinking mindfully about the apparent selfish impulsiveness that gets us into love trouble, consider the self-help advice of taking a "premarital test drive" before committing to marriage. The idea is that living together in a "trial marriage" will help partners discover the nature of real marriage and therefore reduce the risk of divorce. Sixty-two percent of Americans in their twenties think that living together lessens the chances for divorce, yet ten major studies in Europe, Canada, and the United States found that living together increases the chances for divorce.[6]

There are various reasons why cohabitation is a recipe for marital failure. One is a sense of false confidence. Young people living happily together in the fresh but always temporary first bloom of romance say, "We've made it for two years! Marriage should be a snap." But marriage is supposed to be forever; partners should be aware that the excitement that energized those first few years will gradually dim. And, by the way, the dimming is a good thing. Who has the energy and endurance for sixty years of passionate loving? And if we did, how would we have the time and attention to raise children, to be successful members of society, and to savor the natural changes and challenges of a long and fully shared life?

The reality of day-in, day-out life together may come as a shock to the couple who had assumed they were immune to problems because of their romantically charged premarital trial run. The letdown may be more drastic, more insurmountable, to the couple whose confidence was unrealistically high than to the couple expecting trouble.

BLINDED BY THE LIGHT OF YOUR LIFE

As a clinical psychologist in charge of one of the first and largest marital and sexual dysfunction clinics in the world, I encountered the aftermath of love lies every day. As I listened to such comments as "She really turned me on but she changed" or "He made me warm all over and then he cooled off" or "No one had ever made me feel the way she did but she wasn't who I thought she was" or "I thought I had found the one person for me and we'd be together forever," I realized that people were not only mistaking lust for love, but they did not really want to love someone else at all. Self-helpism's focus on adoring and enhancing the self was distracting us from the real source of lasting love. Enduring interpersonal loving relationships are based much less on regard for the self and much more on concern for the relationship.

One woman's statement caused me to wonder whether any of us really has the heart or the mind for lasting love. She had been divorced seven times and was planning to marry a man who, she said, "really lights my fire." She added, "Every man I married was the light of my life, but the light always seemed to go out and I have to light another match. I hope this one stays lit." When I laughed, she was offended. She wasn't joking. She said, "Life is all about love, and I'm not giving up on it." Her statement showed not only how lovers want someone to light up their personal lives instead of someone with whom to share life but also how quickly lovers adapt to losing one flame and start looking for a hotter-burning match.

Many of the unhappy spouses I counseled were looking for "me" therapy, not marital counseling. They were motivated by self-helpism's personal happiness ethic to find partners who would be the "light" of their lives. They had often found partners willing to exchange love lies about becoming one unit forever; but seldom had these spouses made mutual promises to learn how to struggle together through the dark times. Relationships that fail are based on biological attraction and the experience of an enhanced self. The lovers may not have been intentionally lying, but the effect of their passionate pronouncements was to promise what they would never be able to deliver, that is, to maintain an intense, passionate, romantic love until death did them part.

Love is too often an ongoing quest for self-fulfillment. We fail to understand that passion is automatic but that real love is a decision to do lifelong work at becoming caring companions who develop what psychologists call *companionate love*. As George Bernard Shaw wrote in 1903 in *Man and Superman*, "When two people are under the influence of the most violent, most insane, most delusive, and most transient of passions, they are required to swear that they will remain in that excited, abnormal, and exhausting condition continuously until death do them part." Of course, we can't. Passion may spark love, but it isn't love and it can't maintain love. Friedrich Nietzsche described the true nature of lasting love: "It's not the lack of love, but a lack of friendship that makes an unhappy marriage."

BONDING, BOREDOM, AND BLISS

I blame the self-help movement—or at least the Western world's self-esteem worship—for much of the failure of our intimate relationships. In its relentless promotion of self-esteem and its pursuit of personal happiness that is more intense than whatever we have now, self-helpism is offering a recipe for relationship failure; it sees love as another thing to be acquired in the self-fulfilled life, not as a state sufficient and significant unto itself. Even self-helpism's marriage manuals place more emphasis on how partners can get what they want out of the relationship than on how they can contribute to it.

Self-helpism's happiness ethic neglects the scientific research on lasting happiness. For example, psychologists have long known about the "adaptation-level principle." This is our tendency to "get used to"—and bored with—things and people in our environment and then assume that happiness lies just beyond that boredom. We're never satisfied, and maturity requires recognizing that fact, calming down, being less selfish, and accepting our partners for what they are. We quickly establish a "happiness neutral point" and then compare everything else and everyone else against it, and this leads to chronic discontent with our present state of happiness.

Imagine that color television is no longer available. Most of us would be most unhappy with black-and-white television images, and the very young among us could not imagine life without color television. We've adapted to color, and in search of something more exotic than our now neutral experience of color television, we continue to up the ante. We even learn technical language for issues—resolution, surround sound, hi-definition, plasma screen—that did not exist before the advent of the more refined technology. The researcher Richard Ryan wrote, "Satisfaction has a short half-life," and the same applies to our relationships.[7] Until we become more mindful of how love works, we will continue to lie ourselves right out of one of the most essential aspects of being fully alive: the privilege of loving another being till death do us part.

LOVE'S TWO SIDES

Until we approach love more mindfully and with less surrender to hormones and self-enhancement motivation, it is unlikely that marriage will become a more enduring institution. Until parents become more mature companion couples and, in turn, our children learn to care about their parents as much as they do themselves, the younger generation is also unlikely to learn how to love for life. But these young people *will* retain vivid memories of two people who didn't know how to love, couldn't love, were too lazy to learn to love, or were too selfishly busy to care.

An important psychological study offers at least one contrarian way to approach love and illustrates what scientists call the "two-factor" theory of loving, that is, the finding that our emotions have two ingredients—the physical arousal part and the "cognitive appraisal part." For love, this means mindless and mindful love. Psychologist Elaine Hatfield may be less well known than the relationship guru John Grey, the author of *Men Are from Mars, Woman Are from Venus,* but her scientific approach to love offers good ideas for drawing our own mental love maps.

Hatfield's research shows that there are two phases to love: temporary—always temporary—passionate love (primarily physical, self-gratifying, and hormonal) and a more mindful or cognitive love (thinking about how we feel, what and who are making us feel that way, and how we make our partner feel).[8] Her theory and findings have prompted me to tell my students who report that they have "fallen in love" to go somewhere, sit down, wait a few months, and it will pass. I tell them that if they feel turned on, that's the time to calm down and look for ways they can learn to think together. I tell them that my research shows that lovers don't have to be of one mind, but if their loving is to become permanent, they both have to be much more mindful than their hormones and selfish brains drive them to be.

Psychologists Donald Dutton and Arthur Aron studied how powerful "phase one love"—the passionate kind—can be and how it can overwhelm "phase two love," the cognitive kind. They visited two bridges spanning British Columbia's Capilano River.[9] One bridge swayed precariously over the river, but the other was low and firm. As young men walked off the bridges, they were each greeted by an attractive young woman who asked them to fill out a questionnaire about a project she was working on and offered her phone number in case they wanted to know more about what she was doing. Far more of the men who had walked off the swinging bridge with their hearts pounding took her number and called her. As those who go on exciting dates such as sky diving and roller-coaster riding might be aware of, it's not just the date but the adrenaline that makes the heart grow fonder, or at least beat faster. This is not a good—or bad—thing; it simply shows that what we believe are profound instincts are more malleable than we realize.

Other more recent research supports Hatfield's theory that we too easily confuse our emotions with our thoughts. For example, college men were aroused by running in place, viewing erotic material, or listening to funny or repulsive monologues. They were then introduced to an attractive woman and asked to rate her attractiveness. Unlike the control group of men who had not been aroused, these men reported that they thought they had been turned on by the women, not the other stimulation.[10] Self-helpism constantly encourages us to get in touch with our own feelings, but lasting love requires that we get much more in touch with our *thoughts* about our feelings. We love being in the phase one kind of love, but we don't think enough to allow phase two love to develop.

REJECTION SENSITIVITY

All this talk about a more reasonable loving may not sound very romantic, but that's not a bad thing. Research shows that this information is essential to the development of the kind of calm, deep, mutually caring relationship that has a chance of enduring and that enhances the health and well-being of everyone. Researchers Ellen Berscheid and her colleagues studied passionate and compassionate loving and came to this conclusion: "If the inevitable odds against eternal passionate love in a relationship were better understood, more people might choose to be satisfied with the quieter feeling of satisfaction and contentment."[11]

When we think we've finally found someone who makes our "self" happy, we say we are "head over heels" or "crazy in love." We think in the "hot and go" mindless way that prevents us from fully knowing someone. The danger of this self-fulfilling kind of loving is that it can lead to the fear that losing our love object will totally destroy us, a kind of rejection anxiety that prevents the mindful assessment of the relationship.

Psychologists have found that loving "to make the self complete" motivated by what they call "rejection sensitivity" results in a kind of "passion paranoia," the mental and emotional predisposition to expect and constantly look for the slightest sign of the beginning of the end and to react intensely when the flame does flicker.[12]

Love motivated by "rejection sensitivity" is a manifestation of the perpetual adolescence fostered by self-help's lifelong "getting ready to live" approach to life. It renders teenagers daffy. Instead of learning together how to love, one partner becomes ever vigilant for the slightest clue of rejection and the other partner feels pressured to perform or pretend.

A HEALTHY LOVE TRIANGLE

Research shows that a true marriage of consciousness (what one of the couples I treated in my clinic called "mindful merging") is characterized by loving in three dimensions: from the perspective of a child, a parent, and a teenager all rolled into one:

It's vulnerable, childish, and unabashedly codependent loving. It's obedient, deferent, and needy loving. It's loving someone who is willing to ignore our shortcomings and offer us a parental sense of safety, acceptance, guidance, and confidence.

It's the forgiving, parental loving of someone who is loving us childishly and depends on us for safety, acceptance, guidance, and
confidence.

It's an impetuous adolescent loving inspired by the need for intense
physical intimacy that may decrease in frequency but not in its
capacity to induce and rekindle a sense of profound connection.

Research shows that being in a relationship characterized by this
generational triad is a better predictor of happiness than job satisfaction and wealth combined. It provides the best buffer against many of
the effects of poverty, it reduces our chances of getting sick, and it im-
proves our chances for healing when we are seriously ill.[13] We're not
asked about its presence in our lives when we have our annual physical
exam, but perhaps we should be.

Most of us sense that our greatest human strength is our connection
to other humans. Why, then, if this "L" factor is so magnificently powerful, can't we put our minds to our loving? Why do we continue to be,
as author Os Guinness says, living longer but loving more briefly?[14]

TOO SELFISH FOR LASTING LOVE?

Each year in the United States, there are about 2.4 million marriages
and 1.2 million divorces. These figures do not count the breakups of
the increasingly prevalent cohabiting couples, nor do they take into
account the fact that fewer people are marrying in the first place. In
1960, about 25 percent of American adults were single. Today, that
percentage has risen to almost 50 percent. As I have pointed out, the
epidemic of disconnection may be related at least in some measure to
the fact that today's relationships are composed of persons raised in the
climate of self-helpism. Two self-potential-seeking partners may never
equal a relationship that has the potential to last.

Self-help's encouragement of an innate narcissism and general pessimism regarding the human psyche leads to advice from the likes of self-helper John Bradshaw, who wrote, "There is no human security. There is no one who will always take care us."[15] His comment reflects the selfish approach to love. His message ignores and even berates those who love to take care of others and love being taken care of in return. Perhaps because of the dominance of his own quest for self-fulfillment, he can't imagine someone willing to be selfless enough to fulfill a pledge to care for him forever. If he did, it is likely he would see that person as suffering from the dreaded self-help disease of co-dependence and the caretaking lover as an enabler.

Self-help is almost totally pessimistic about the possibility of lasting love and easily accepts failed relationships; it sees divorce not as failure but as a sign of personal growth in the ever-developing self. Self-help is dedicated to fixing relationships that it assumes will be broken. Just as with most areas of our lives, self-help is pathology-focused and looks for what is *wrong* with our love. Its various programs offer ways to "fight fair" and to "resolve conflict," not how to find what's *right* about our loving and learn how to enhance it.

OPPOSITES DISTRACT

In the typical "we-can-fix-anything" orientation of self-helpism, the marriage expert George Levinger made this assertion: "What counts in making a happy marriage is not so much how compatible you are, but how you deal with incompatibility."[16] His optimism exceeds what research on marriage promises. When we're selecting a partner for life, we are wise to remember that similarity breeds contentment. Starting off marriage with the idea that opposites attract imposes a tremendous burden on both partners no matter how much self-help advice is available for "working it out."

Compatibility has been shown to be crucial for a lasting relationship.[17] Stories about opposites attracting are just that, stories. They tell of all sorts of creatures with totally opposite characteristics and temperaments living in harmonious unity, like Frog and Toad in Arnold Lobel's books; but in real life, similarity matters. The famous journalist Walter Lippmann was in line with scientific findings when he pointed out that love tends to last "when lovers love many things together, and not merely each other." Assuming incompatibility and then focusing on trying to fix it may sell self-help books, but better advice might be "think of similarity first." In the difficult challenge of learning how to love for life, we don't need the distraction of being incompatible in the first place.

PROPOSITIONS OF LOVE

Here are some of my own propositions on love for your consideration. They run contrary to what you may have read or heard from self-helpism, but landmark studies on love like those mentioned above suggest they are worth your and your partner's attention.

Love Proposition #1: You have to learn to love others before you can love yourself.   As you have read, the central assumption of self-helpism is that well-being is primarily a personal task. This perspective maintains that, to paraphrase coach Vince Lombardi's famous remark, self-esteem isn't everything—it's the only thing.

It's true that we all have a deep need to love ourselves, but we also have an equally strong and—as parental love indicates—even stronger drive to connect. A mindful approach to loving is to focus on strengthening a relationship that we hold in even higher esteem than we hold ourselves. Self-helpism looks for problems within one person, but it is ultimately in our *relationships* that health and happiness reside.[18]

Putting in the effort to focus on loving one person in a committed relationship full of the foibles and frustrations of daily living may be more demanding than trying to love ourselves, but its joy and benefits are immense, not only for those who find it but for those who are found. Self-helpers accept the idea that the first step to saying "I love you" is to focus on the "I," not the "you." Self-awareness and personal authenticity are essential for maturity, but that awareness cannot be found in a vacuum. We know ourselves only by knowing others; the "I" and the "you" are equally important to "love."

The most enduring love is a two-person event. It comes alive from the union of a mother and the child in her womb. Ask any mother and she will tell you that she loved her child long before its birth and that her loving bond with that child is infinite. The newborn may not be able to conceptualize love, but the baby experiences life with whatever consciousness she or he has in the context of total committed dependence on another being. I suggest that we begin life as two people, not one, and that the quest for "self-actualization" and an ever more highly esteemed self is doing as much harm as good.

The Hawaiian legend of the *naupaka* flower says that when two young lovers were separated, the maiden took a flower from behind her ear and tore it in half. Her tears stained the flower's petals, and to this day, we can see her tiny teardrops on the blossoms. She gave one half of the flower to her lover when he was banished forever to the mountains, and placed the other half back behind her ear to wear as she went to live forever by the sea. Now, when the *naupaka* flower blooms in the bright Hawaiian sun, it does so in the mountains and by the sea. This legend represents a love sustained by the knowledge that none of us is ever really self-fulfilled until we have learned the loving act of selfless permanent connection.

Love Proposition #2: True love is not emotional; it's volitional. Chaucer's famous words, "Love is blynd," refer to the thoughtless infatuation of the self with a love object that somehow enhances that self. This is the kind of loving in which we mistake the arousing state of emotional infatuation with the mental, emotional, physical, and spiritual effort required to establish, maintain, and grow a lasting bond. Love is as much a matter of the mind as it is the heart.

When we pair up more for a sense of increased self-esteem than to commit to the creation of a new "us" way of living, we reap what we sow. It is no coincidence that divorce occurs most frequently after about three years of marriage, the duration of emotional and physical infatuation. This is when we need to think more about the relationship, not abandon it.[19] It may be wiser not to marry when you think you are in love, but instead when you feel ready to learn to love marriage. Rather than trying to scratch what the poet W. H. Auden called that "intolerable neural itch," we need to calm down and *think*.

Lasting love requires that we make a mental choice, not yield to a physiological response. Love is based more on mindful "cool and know" mutual thought than "hot and go" individual thinking. In words that will make self-helpers cringe, love is a form of mutual dependence through which both partners make a mental and emotional contract to grow and learn together rather than just individually climb the steps to their own self-actualization.

Love Proposition #3: Enduring love is conditional, not unconditional. Another self-help principle of love is that it should be unconditional. This has increasingly become a way of loving that excuses inconsiderate or selfish behavior, and it leads to a lack of loving responsibility. It's my view that all love, both the love we hope to receive and the love we choose to invest in, should be conditional upon demonstrated loving behavior and not just upon promises or apologies.

To paraphrase Forrest Gump, love is as love does. The self-help belief is that we behave as we feel, but we can also come to feel as we behave.

You have control over your behavior and thus over your emotions. There are two sides to this issue. Some people believe they have moral choices other than to love their partners no matter what; others believe that they deserve love, no matter how they behave. I say that both are wrong.

I've noticed that many men and women who say they love their partners appear to treat complete strangers with more respect and common good manners than they show their partners. I am stunned that so many women and men tolerate abusive treatment or engage in it themselves yet still say they love their partners.

We don't deserve love, we earn it. The conditions of being loved include how caringly we speak, how openly we listen, how far we go out of our way to help, how much time we spend on growing a relationship, and how much personal responsibility we take for the quality of the relationship and our partner's life. It may be romantic to sit by candlelight staring longingly into each other's eyes, but sitting with your partner watching a television show you absolutely hate just because she or he enjoys that show more when you're there is the kind of behavior that is the basis for conditional love.

Being loveable comes before being loved. Don't wait to fall in love; start loving by putting your behavior where your heart is. Anyone who does not continually try to earn love doesn't deserve it. The key question to me is not "Am I in love?" but "Am I behaving in a love-worthy way?"

Love Proposition #4: Healthy love is a matter of being the right partner, not finding the right person. "Would you want to be married to you?" I have found that a carefully considered and sincerely positive answer to this question can be a good predictor of the ability to sustain love. It means that true love is not a matter of searching until we find our one and only love match; true love is accepting the challenge of *being* the kind of person with whom you yourself would want to spend a lifetime.

THE LOVE-WORTHY TEST

Here's a little quiz to see whether you are loving in accordance with my fourth proposition about love. Although the questions may at first appear to derive from the typical "what's in it for me" orientation, they are intended to encourage you to think about how your own behavior impacts your partner. As you answer each one, think of how your own behavior influences the "love ecology" of your relationship. Put a check mark by the items to which you answer a confident "yes."

1. _____ Are you clear about how much appreciation your partner needs you to show, and do you keep working to show it even if you don't understand why he or she needs it so much?

2. _____ Do you defer to your partner's "housework help" criteria by doing more even though you think you already do more than your fair share?

3. _____ Do you "stifle yourself" by not saying what you feel like saying because you think it might hurt your partner's feelings?

4. _____ Do you acknowledge and try to live up to your partner's ideas about personal hygiene practices even though they are not the same as yours and even seem silly?

5. _____ Do you try to dress in ways that please your partner even though you would sooner wear something else?

6. _____ Do you try to live up to your partner's definition of punctuality?

7. _____ Are you willing to talk on your partner's terms by listening as long as he or she wants and talking about what he or she wants to talk about, even if it requires you to draw on your entire store of energy, attention, and ability to mask boredom?

8. _____ Do you do things (such as shopping, watching sports, yard work) just because your partner loves doing them and enjoys them more when you do them with her or him?

9. ____ Do you avoid correcting your partner even when you easily and rightly could?

10. ____ Do you pay attention to being a good sleeping partner by sacrificing the sheets, not rolling over because you might wake your partner, turning off the light or television even when you would sooner leave them on, and trying to go to bed and get up in synch with your partner?

11. ____ Do you know what makes your partner laugh, try to cheer him or her up when you can, and laugh at your partner's jokes even when you've heard them many times before?

12. ____ Are you cautious with your comments and jokes even though you think your partner is oversensitive on some issues? (The AT&T rule of marital humor: Is your joke Appropriate, Timely, and Tasteful—by your partner's standards, not yours?)

13. ____ Have you asked about your partner's sexual preferences and turn-offs (not assumed them), and do you try to comply with them?

14. ____ Do you "lie" well to your partner by complimenting cooking or projects that you really consider a disaster?

15. ____ Do you think your partner would eagerly marry you again?

_____ TOTAL "YES" ANSWERS

The more "yes" answers you had to these fifteen questions, the more likely it is that you are being love-worthy. I used this Love-Worthy test in my own research on couples who attended some of my lectures. From the 173 couples for whom I could get follow-up data, 58 ended up separated or divorced. Their joint scores on the Love-Worthy tests were all lower than 15. Just thinking and talking with your partner from the perspective suggested by these questions might help you both begin to form the connective dialogue that leads to lasting love. Perhaps then you can savor the benefits that come from holding your relationship in higher esteem than you hold yourself.

None of us is or probably ever will be loved in the exact way we want to be loved. If we hope to develop a more loving, lasting, and fulfilling relationship, the first step is to put our focus on our own love-worthiness by being the right partner, not trying to find one.

Love Proposition #5: Lasting love is based on mutual delusion. Anyone who is married is married to a fool and so is his or her spouse. If love is going to last between two imperfect people whose faults will become more evident as time passes and the euphoria of passion subsides, each partner must be willing to indulge in self-deception about the true nature of the other. Enduring love requires that both partners be willing to blind themselves to the annoying flaws and failings we all bring to our relationships.

Research shows that the bigger the discrepancy between the more objective view that friends may have of your partner and your own more favorable illusion about your partner's foibles and eccentricities, the more the chance for lasting love.[20] For example, I knew a couple who appeared to be mismatched: The wife was a sunny person who saw the bright side of everything, but the husband, though witty and kindhearted, could only be described as a curmudgeon. If she said the sun was sure to come out, he packed an umbrella; where she saw their children engaged in creative artwork, he saw a mess in the living room. When one of her friends finally asked her how she bore up under his negative outlook, she chirped, "Oh, he's happy—in his own way. That's just how he shows it."

New research shows that couples who engage in the biggest illusions regarding each other's faults tend to be the most happy and long-loving couples. Lasting love involves the ability to see virtues in our partners that just aren't there. Over time, these loving illusions have a positive side effect: Our partners may actually try to live up to them.

Martin Seligman, the positive psychologist pioneer, describes loving illusion as the "yes, but" approach to love.[21] Unlike unconditional loving, partners who engage in this kind of "yes, but" thinking don't just go along with annoying partner behaviors by saying they "love them anyway." Instead, they show the will to maintain the relationship despite these faults and the wisdom to reframe and qualify them more positively.

My wife is a world-class love illusionist. Living with me has required it. One of my faults is my impatience and irritation with people who appear to be leading their lives mindlessly. I'm sure friends recognize my mindless hot-and-go thinking, but my wife uses the "yes, but" approach. She says, "Sure, Paul reacts quickly, but he sees the potential in people to act more kindly than they do." Sure enough, I've found myself at least trying to reduce my intolerant impatience and to live up to my wife's loving illusion.

Growing relationships involve partners who, consciously or unconsciously, conspire together to create a collaborative illusion about each other's strengths and weaknesses. They manufacture a set of delusions that provide a love map for each person toward behaving more in accordance with the illusions they have created for each other.

Instead of seeing your partner for "what he or she really is," try to see what that person can be and make an effort to be what he or she sees in you whether it is there or not. At least sometimes, our partners can surprise us by making our deluded dreams about them come true, and making dreams come true together is perhaps the truest and most enduring way to love.

Committed to a Family Asylum

If you have never been hated by your child,
you have never been a parent.

BETTE DAVIS

PROPOSITIONS ABOUT "FAMILYING"

1. Adult behavior is not caused by childhood experiences.
2. Parenting seldom works, but "familying" does.
3. Children are not our most precious resource.
4. Good parents don't worry about their children's self-esteem.
5. Children don't deserve a better life than we had.

DELIGHTFULLY DYSFUNCTIONAL

Do you come from a weird family? Does your family yell, argue, even fight? Do you have at least one family member who would immediately be voted out were it not for unbreakable family ties? Have you ever fantasized about running away from your family?

If you answered yes to these questions, congratulations! Your family is absolutely normal, delightfully dysfunctional, and doing what families are supposed to do: provide a safe place for naturally flawed beings to sleep, eat, grow, learn, fail, flourish, and act in ways that no one outside the family would tolerate.

The best definition of a family I've been able to come up with is this: "A group of two or more people irrationally committed to one another's welfare." The best definition of a home is Robert Frost's: "Home is the place where, when you go there, they have to take you in."

I like these definitions because they focus on the idea that a family is *supposed* to be dysfunctional. Families are society's way of providing mini mental institutions, family asylums to which we allow ourselves to be voluntarily committed.

This idea of the family as a refuge comes from a way of thinking about family that I call "familism," or a way of living in which family solidarity, tradition, and caring take on greater value than individual interests. Familism is the perfect antidote to the self-obsession pervading our society, but it does *not* mean putting the needs of any one person—child, mother, or father—over the needs of another. Just as I value the connection between two people in a loving relationship more than the individual self-interest of each person, familism values the strength of the family as a whole over the self-interest of everyone in it.

SAFETY IN THE MADHOUSE

Although I have suggested that intimate love between two adults should be conditional, strong families are distinguished by their unique brand of *un*conditional acceptance of their members or fellow inmates. As those who have experienced the most dreadful treatment from a family member or observed his or her terrible behavior know, that person is forever a family member and nothing will change that. In all family situations, you accept the hand you were dealt and then move on. I don't suggest that anyone should try to maintain a relationship with a chronically abusive parent, for example. But it is pointless to deny that parent's existence and importance in our lives.

Once we're born, adopted, married, or otherwise merged into what we consider to be our family, we are committed for life to this often bizarre but strongest of all of society's institutions. And in lesser cases of family mistreatment—the kind we've all experienced, the kind that comes only from knowing one another too well—the power of family bonds can be astounding. They are sustained less by logic than by love.

Unconditional family love doesn't excuse destructive behavior, but it allows for behavioral limit-testing. Bad behavior is not excused, or even necessarily understood, but persistent, even unreasonable, love is the specialty of the family. Society needs a place where someone cares no matter what. From the small child who bites to the teenager who steals and the parent who looks for emotional support from his children rather than the other way around, every member has something to learn and something to gain from the support of the family.

Self-help's dreaded "dysfunction" is not a bad thing. Every family I know, including my own, is probably dysfunctional by self-help standards. We all quarrel, we behave childishly and dependently, we take way too long to grow up, we throw tantrums. But we are all family and we have at least one member with whom any rational adult would not want to spend much time. But we get what we need from one another: patience, instruction, stability, someone to talk to and listen to, and, most of all, to love. One person's dysfunction is another's opportunity for growth. Without the practice of dealing with the misbehavior of our family members, none of us would have the tolerance essential for a gentle and caring society. The family, far from perfect as it is, provides an emotional safe house for troubled souls.

FAMILIES AREN'T FOR CHILDREN

Contrary to popular opinion, families aren't places designed exclusively as training academies for the development of smart and talented children. The purpose of a family is not to produce happy children but to produce loving interdependent responsible adults who hold others in higher esteem than they do themselves.

The family is the crucible where individual weaknesses and strengths can be forged into a whole stronger than the sum of its parts. A family is not just a child daycare center but the center of care for everyone who belongs to it, and that's what makes families such a wonderfully frustrating and demanding challenge.

Families are places where all the family members can learn the essential skill of selfless commitment to a purpose higher than themselves, the purpose of loving connection. It's where excellence can be defined not by individual goals but by mutually shared objectives. It's where members learn interdependence and, yes, even codependence, so that its younger members can go on to love others and begin the challenging task of extending the family.

THE PROBLEM AND PRIVILEGE OF PARENTING

If we are not fully ready for it, one of the worst things that can happen to us is to have a child. Fortunately, it can also be one of the best things. Whether raising children feels like the highest privilege or the most nagging burden depends on whether we want to develop our children or want to develop *with* our children. A fact of parental life is that regardless of parenting technique, selfish people make lousy parents and raise even more self-involved children.

According to the "how to do it" books on parenting, raising children has become less of a family celebration than another task to be mastered and another set of activities to be scheduled. Self-helpism converted the noun "parent" into a verb that refers to a set of steps and programs to be learned. Instead of giving our children life models, parenting has come to mean providing every possible opportunity for children to express themselves.

"Parenting" is often another opportunity on the self-help menu that might lead to the ever-illusive self-fulfillment through the "having a child" experience. As a result of this self-enhancing view of the adult-child relationship, parenting can become a project more than a sacred privilege. Self-help's "good life ethic" and constant pursuit of more and more happiness leads to the belief that our parental self-esteem rests with our capacity to see that our children have a better life than we had.

I wonder whether the "better life" that parents hope for their children will be even faster paced and more disconnected than their own? Parents would be wiser to show that they have a loving life worth emulating, that they are not consumed by the pursuit of a better one either for themselves or their children. The greatest gift parents can give their children is the message that they are savoring their own good life together right now.

FAMILY LESSONS FROM THE IRON MAIDEN

The belief that families—and parents in particular—have a profound yet all but unknowable power over their children's future has deep roots in our society. From a few nuggets of science, the self-help industry built a solid gold fortress of belief bias about how parents' treatment of their children reverberates throughout the ages.

One well-known study appears to uphold this idea. Perhaps nothing more clearly demonstrated the intensity of the need for parental love than Harry Harlow's work with macaque monkeys and what he called his Iron Maiden.

Harlow was a famous—some would say infamous—psychologist who studied love, contact comfort, and other aspects of loving connection by having baby monkeys bond with surrogate mothers instead of real monkey mothers. He constructed "mother figures" from wire and terry cloth.[1] He discovered that infant monkeys cared more for this soft surrogate than a metal but tasty milk-bearing fake mother. Love grew from soft touch, not from good taste, and the term "contact comfort" was coined.

Coming at a time (in the late 1940s and early 1950s) when behaviorism's strict "punishment-reward" approach to parenting was in its prime, the idea that love occurred even without the reward of mother's milk was revolutionary. But Harlow wanted to know more about the power of love, and so he made what he called the Iron Maiden. Unlike the first metal, milk-bearing mothers and the terry cloth surrogate mothers that the monkeys cuddled lovingly even when no milk was provided, the Iron Maiden version wasn't so comforting.

Iron Maiden Mom was abusive. She was made of hard cold metal and her sharp spikes shot blasts of frigid air that sent the baby monkeys flying back and away to be slammed against the bars of the cage. (It's not hard to understand why Harlow's reputation as an animal abuser began during this period of his work.) Some of his Iron Maidens shot cold water over their monkey babies, and some even stabbed them, but the babies came back for more of the only contact they could get from the only mother they knew. The loving they sought nearly killed them, but they persisted in their attachment to this brutal stepmother.

The surrogate-raised monkeys went into their adolescence ill prepared to love, to mate, to socialize, or to be content. They would sit for hours in their cages screaming, slamming the walls of the cage, and even eating their fingers in frustration. If ever we needed proof that early maltreatment was damaging, here it was.

But it is dangerous to extrapolate too much from these early find-ings—and that is exactly what the self-helpers have done. Harlow's work told us three things: One, that terrible abuse from an early age can have lasting effects; two, that infants need gentleness even more than they need nourishment; and three, that a primate instinct to re-turn to the family, no matter how terrible that family has been, always exists. Yet the "common wisdom" propagated in the self-help era is that *any dysfunction of adulthood can be traced to childhood trauma*. This is simply lazy thinking, and it has nothing to do with science.

Self-helpism persists in the belief that families are hotbeds for all sorts of terrible repressed memories caused by terrible parents who produced generations of damaged inner children left to wander the aisles of bookstore self-help sections in search of a "home." When we seek to find ourselves through isolated self-actualization and freedom from our families, we end up distracted from the cultural origins and sense of belonging that serve as a spiritual base.

TOO MUCH CREDIT, TOO MUCH BLAME

Most of us were not neglected or wounded by our parents. They may have made mistakes, and sometimes some big ones that we may still re-call with pain and even resentment, but most of us still hold mostly lov-ing memories of our lives with them. They may not have done the best, but we believe they tried their best.

Research shows, however, that our parents don't deserve all the credit they get when we do wonderful things, nor do they deserve the blame for our current feelings or problems. I worry that all the self-help talk about wounding fragile children exaggerates the impact of in-evitable natural parental mistakes and causes parents to make more mistakes than they would because they're trying so hard not to mess up their kids. This exaggeration also dangerously trivializes the brutality of real abuse.

The researchers Robert Plomin and Denise Daniels have studied hundreds of siblings. They wrote, "Two children in the same family are on average as different from one another as are pairs of children selected randomly from the population."[2] Most parents with more than one child have often wondered whether there wasn't some mistake made at the hospital. Were we given a child from a totally different family—or planet? One of our kids runs recklessly into the ocean, but the other has to be dragged to the water's edge to test the water with her toe. Same family, same parents, yet the children have completely different temperaments.

Self-helpism has tended to adopt what the psychologist and researcher Michael Gazzaniga called a "cruel extreme environmentalism" in which parents are convinced that anything and everything they do or don't do is contributing to another damaged inner child.[3] Well-meaning and frustrated parents, take heart. Research shows that it takes years of constant effort to mess up our kids.

RESILIENT TWIGS

Summarizing his research on child development, Martin Seligman wrote, "If you want to blame your parents for your own adult problems, you are entitled to blame the genes they gave you, but you are not entitled—by any facts I know—to blame the way they treated you. . . . We are not prisoners of our past."[4]

Self-help's childhood history bias can be traced back to Sigmund Freud's belief that our adult problems are caused by our childhood experiences. Although Freud is often credited with saying that "the child is father to the man," it was actually the poet William Wordsworth who said that, and he may have been echoing Alexander Pope's famous statement, "Just as the twig is bent, the tree's inclin'd."[5] When Pope made this statement about the flexibility of twigs, he was talking about educational systems and their impact on children, not parenting. Even if we apply Pope's growing tree analogy to family life, the fact is that new tree sprouts are bent by years of consistent pressure from other trees, rocks, and wind. In this sense, we really are like twigs and have an innate psychological trajectory to grow upright and right. In summarizing research on the impact of parenting on children, the psychologist Robyn Dawes wrote, "Only continual obstacles will prevent an initial bend in a twig from righting itself in the direction of the sunlight."[6]

I'd love to take credit for my son Scott's gentle patience and immense courage in the face of his cerebral palsy, but I know better. He's been a kind and strong person from the moment he was born. I often blame myself for not being able, despite my best efforts, to find someone or something that could help our adopted son Roger's struggles with his severe learning disability, but he saw things differently from the time he could first tell us what he saw. I love them both dearly, but I'm not at all sure how much our best efforts to parent well helped or hurt them. I do know that research shows that at least 50 percent of who and how we are is genetically determined, so we do come out of the womb "pre-bent"; our environment as determined by our parents might help bend us a little more one way or another, but really not nearly enough that their actions will determine most of our conduct as adults.

LOST CHILDREN

An episode of the PBS show *Frontline* chronicled the trials of Rockdale County, Georgia, and the story illustrates my belief that adolescent and adult misery does not stem from parental mistreatment.

The program reported that in the years between 1996 and 1999, a small middle-class Georgia county experienced several tragedies. A sixteen-year-old boy was killed in a fight at a shopping mall parking lot.

Another teenager shot six fellow students at a local high school. Seventeen teenagers, ages fourteen to seventeen, tested positive for syphilis, and two hundred others had been exposed to it. When the health department investigated the syphilis outbreak, it discovered that group sex and alcohol and drug abuse were rampant among even the youngest teens.

The parents of these teenagers were highly successful and financially secure, but constantly busy and distracted. They were good people who were working hard to give their children an even better existence than they already had. They cared about their children and were busy trying to parent to the best of their ability. They weren't abusive or neglectful; many of these parents devoted all their free time to their children's school and extracurricular activities. Their parenting skills appeared to be in excellent shape—but their familying skills were sorely lacking.

Commenting on these lost children of Rockdale County, the sociologist Michael Resnik said there was "a fundamental emptiness" there.[7] He noted streets lined with expensive but empty houses and the absence of any real connection between the adults who had mortgaged them and the children who were only visiting them. Like their parents, the young people were unconnected to anything other than the pursuit of "raw and relentless" pleasure and fulfillment of the self. They weren't abused in the way self-helpers suggest, but they were deprived of the chance to witness and experience love in progress.

Like Harry Harlow's baby monkeys who took the milk they needed from a metal "mom" but clung to the cloth-covered statue for comfort, these children were living proof that material comfort is not enough. They were getting their "milk"—their cars, immaculate homes, fashionable clothes, and expensive summer camps—but they were not getting that all-important connective love, the kind that can be found within strong families. And disaster was the result.

GROWING DOWN INSTEAD OF UP

The behavior of the parents of Rockdale County can hardly be singled out as a dreadful exception to the rule. All over the country, adults are acting more and more like children—self-interested, self-involved.

The self-help movement values "growing down." It stresses a perpetual "me first" immaturity that morphs into a lifelong self-indulgence of prolonged adolescence. If we have failed at all as parents, our failure is that our children are becoming too much "just like us," mini-self-potentialists in relentless pursuit of their own happiness above all else. We haven't produced damaged inner children, but we are producing damaged real children who are as discontented as we are. In part because of self-help's belief bias in favor of the "within," we have neglected the "between."

I recently observed a self-help seminar that encouraged doctors, lawyers, politicians, and business executives to "find their self-potential" by behaving like children. With the encouragement of their leader, they hopped, skipped, jumped, shook tambourines, blew whistles, shot one another with Nerf guns, and screamed. "Let your inner child out. Let him play with life and be free to be all he can be!" yelled the seminar leader, who had a red bulb stuck on her nose. "Never grow up. Let your emotions free. See your world through the eyes of your child within! That's where all creativity rests."

There is no doubt that play and free self-expression have their place. Living a life without laughter and childishly regressive glee is not only boring but potentially lethal to our physical and mental health. Working too hard, too long, to be always "grown up" can lead to chronic stress. However, the idea that a free-roaming and self-indulgent inner child is the ultimate state of human development will lead to a world populated only by big and little versions of prepubescents never quite able to "find themselves."

There does come a time when we should behave like grown-ups and make that stage so appealing to our children that they are eager to join us instead of making fun of us. When we tell them that we want them to have better lives than we have, are we telling them that we're not all that happy with our own lives? Are we sending them a signal that says they are limiting our happiness? Don't our children need most of all to see and to be raised by parents who are happy with the life they are sharing? The key question in parenting is this: "Would you want your children to be just like you when they grow up?" Would you want them to work, live, enjoy their lives, and treat others just as you do?

Perhaps one reason so many kids are sullen and behave as if they were unparented and undisciplined little adults is that they feel more adored than maturely loved by an adult worth emulating. They watch as their parents cling to youth and chase self-esteem instead of relishing maturity and caring for others.

Parents today spend a lot of time trying to do "for" their children instead of being really "with" them in the process of learning to live in the world. To be good parents, we first have to escape from our own childhoods long enough to help our children learn how to negotiate theirs.

THE QUESTION OF A LIFETIME

One of the most comprehensive studies on the impacts of early life experience and stress was conducted over several decades on students at Harvard University.[8] The key factor that predicted early death in this group was the lack of a *parental loving imprint*. More than any other variable, it was the answer to the question that predicted a long life or an early death: "Did your parents seem to love and respect each other and show it?" Students who used caring, positive words to describe the nature of their parents' relationship lived longer and healthier lives than students who did not.

Although our fate is not sealed by bad parenting, our overall health and chances for a longer life are clearly enhanced when we live under the influence of two people who are in love. Once again, instead of focusing so obsessively on the terrible things that might have happened, we should really be looking at the possibly wonderful things that did happen. Sometimes even the worst family problems are not as bad as TV talk shows make them out to be.

I've been talking a lot about the value of a loving parental bond as a gift to our children, but an example of how a terrible family situation was transcended by a loving parental bond came from a single mother I saw in my clinic. She was continuing to raise her children alone after her husband's death. Both she and her former husband had abused drugs, and their daughters had done more to raise their parents than their parents had done to raise them. But despite their parents' drug abuse, there was a bond between them that left a permanent love imprint on the daughters' souls.

When I interviewed one of the daughters, I was surprised when this seventeen-year-old said, "My mom and dad loved each other. You could see it through all the other crap, and that's what counts for me. I will never forget seeing my mom wiping my dad's forehead and helping him eat when he got real sick. I saw my dad hugging my mom and needing her, and she needed him, too. I saw them cry together for one another, and my sister and I could see how much they loved each other, and that's what we remember most. We don't want to ever go through what my parents did, but we both want to be married like they were and give our kids that kind of memory."

A loving role model like this can provide an emotional boost—a kind of "love-bond buffer"—against the tribulations of daily life. I still find great comfort and direction in my own family life from my memories of my own parents' loving of each other. It has always served as a tenderness template that provides a guide for my own marriage.

THE DECISION TO DIVORCE

I have seen that single parents can do an amazing and courageous job of raising healthy and happy kids, but I am now convinced that no amount of parenting skill can replace the added developmental bonus of growing up in a home with two consistently loving parents who share the privilege of developing with their children. This model is difficult to attain when we so strongly emphasize "self" over "us" help. I wonder whether the preponderance of single parenting and the fact that three out of four children do not grow up in a two-parent home may be directly related to the priority we have come to assign to self-happiness over parental responsibility. A little more guilt about not taking the time to make and stay in a loving relationship may not be a bad thing.

Although an individual sometimes has no option left but to end a marital relationship and try to raise children from that relationship alone, the emphasis placed on fulfilling the self first at almost any cost nonetheless causes children to come second. "Staying together for the children" is now seen as the wrong reason to stay married. Research shows that staying together may be worth more consideration not only for the children but for the ultimate health and well-being of the parents themselves.

The research of the negative impacts of divorce on all persons involved is clear. Divorce is not just "another thing" that happens on the path to self-discovery and personal esteem-building; it's a terrible thing. No adult or child should have to go through it. I agree with David Myers, who summarized his research on the impact of divorce this way: "Divorce is like having a leg amputated. It's bad news, the remedy of last resort, and something we all hope to avoid. But sometimes it's better than keeping the hopeless diseased limb."[9]

The research clearly shows that dual parenting is better for children than single parenting.[10] This is not because single parents love their children any less than married parents; it's because the focus on fulfilling their own potential and doing what they decided was best for themselves contributed to their choice to stop trying to make a relationship work. As a result, their love is stretched thin by the pressures of doing alone what most married parents find difficult enough to do together.

This may sound old-fashioned or "conservative." But my own experience and the current research shows that staying together for the children and putting the self second is not nearly as destructive to either the parent or the child as self-potentialists warn. To those who say they can't possibly stay together because of the constant arguing, I suggest they put in the effort to try to shut up, grow up, and stop fighting. I ask them to ask themselves whether they have not placed representing and standing up for themselves above valuing the intact family.

PROPOSITIONS ABOUT FAMILYING

Familism Proposition Number One: Parenting seldom works, but "familying" always does.   "Parenting" is another invention of the human potential movement, but it is a creation of popular psychology and not a real process. There is no one set of tried-and-true principles for being a good parent, but there are some ideas that can lead to a healthier way of "familying":

- No family will be happier than or more loving than the relationship of the adults within it.
- Everyone in the family must care for one another and show that caring no matter what.
- Connection is not condoning. No matter what a family member does, he or she is family forever.
- Children have as much responsibility to parents as parents have to their children.
- All families are dysfunctional. That's what they're for, to serve as asylums where the weird, stressed, frightened, insecure, and

occasionally obnoxious (which is all of us) can go at night without fear of being kicked out to wander the streets.

• All family members owe their allegiance not to their self-potential
but to the potential of the family to thrive though crises and
savor the good times as a loving group made stronger by their
shared pain.

*Familism Proposition Number Two: Adult behavior is not caused
by childhood experiences.*   A classic study into human resilience by
researchers Emmy Werner and Ruth Smith demonstrated that despite
horrendous family-life experiences, many children turn out just fine.[11]
During the years from 1955 to 1979, Werner and Smith studied a vulnerable group of seven hundred children who grew up in troubled
times in my home state of Hawaii. The influence of the arrival of thousands of newcomers to the islands during the war in Southeast Asia resulted in changes in neighborhoods and people who had little
understanding of the host culture and often little regard for it. Many of
the children Werner and Smith studied came from broken homes and
were raised by single parents who struggled with poverty, substance
abuse, and depression. Although some of the children in this study did
develop later psychological and behavioral problems, many from the
worst situations did not. Werner and Smith summarized their findings
by saying that many of the Kauai children from bad home situations developed into competent and autonomous adults.

The most comprehensive research on the childhood history bias I
could find was done by the psychologists Sandra Scarr, Deborah
Phillips, and Kathleen McCartney.[12] Summarizing child development
data and their analysis of case histories, they agreed with the findings
about the surprisingly resilient nature of children in the face of the
most deleterious experiences. Pointing out that only the most pervasive
and continuous detrimental experiences were likely to have a lasting ef-

fect, they concluded that the "romance of early experience" was not supported by the data and that "continuity does not imply inevitability."

Another study on the childhood history bias was conducted by the psychologist Cathy Widom.[13] To compare a group of children who were abused or neglected by age eleven with children of a similar socioeconomic background whose parents had never been suspected of abuse or neglect, she examined approximately 2,600 petitions involving alleged child abuse or neglect. She then looked at court records for evidence of arrests in the following twenty years. She wrote: "In comparison to controls, abused and neglected children had overall more arrests as a juvenile (26 percent versus 17 percent), more arrests as an adult (29 percent versus 21 percent), and more arrests for any violent offense (11 percent versus 8 percent)."[14]

Widom's study was hailed as proof of the belief bias that abusive parenting leads to antisocial behavior, but she also pointed out in the same study that "the *majority* of abused and neglected children *do not* become delinquent, criminal, or violent."[15] [Italics added.] As you can see from the percentages in Widom's study, almost two-thirds of the abused children *did not* end up committing criminal acts as adults.

More attention to forming a loving bond from which our children can learn, more effort to learn to love when we don't provide that model, and more attention paid to better homemaking (in the broadest and most meaningful sense of that phrase) instead of providing "growth opportunities" are goals worthy of our mindful parental consideration."[16]

Familism Proposition Number Three: Children are not our most precious resource.   Our most important social resource is *not* our children. It is two adults behaving selflessly and teaching their children the same way of altruistic loving. No society will be stronger than its parents' ability to teach and model a connective love over constant self-enhancement.

The elevation of children to the foremost focus of family life does them a major disservice. It can put enormous pressure on them by making it appear that their success dictates the happiness of their parents and the entire family group. It can deny them the opportunity to learn interdependence, the joy of empathy, forgiveness, and the humbleness essential to being able to enter into a lasting loving bond later in their lives. I have found it helpful to think of my role as a parent as one through which I am constantly teaching my sons how to be loving parents themselves. My wife and I have tried to teach them that a loving, enduring relationship is life's most important resource.

Familism Proposition Number Four: Good parents don't worry about their children's self-esteem.   As I have noted throughout this book, the claims of the self-esteem movement are highly overrated. But even though there is not a shred of evidence to support them, more than three hundred states have written more than 170 statutes that codify the promotion of self-esteem.[17] We have come to accept self-potentialism's "hubris equals happiness" equation, and not surprisingly, the result is a society full of narcissists focused almost exclusively on how they feel and how to feel better. Research has shown that the self-esteem movement has put too much emphasis on the self and our regard for it. The psychologist Roy Baumeister has conducted more studies on self-esteem than any other researcher I know of. He wrote: "The enthusiastic claims of the self-esteem movement mostly range from fantasy to hogwash."[18]

Baumeister found in his research that those with the highest self-esteem were often also those who were more likely to be obnoxious, to interrupt, and to lecture people instead of speaking to them with respect (a skill learned at a calm family dinner). Some of the world's worst villains have had "high-self esteem." Violent gang leaders usually think highly of themselves, and some of the current rogues in the growing gallery of corporate corruption, who have been strong advocates of self-potentialism and personal power seminars, have recently demonstrated the perils of relentlessly high self-esteem.

The self-help answer to all this is that those who do wrong may *appear* to have high self-regard but they really suffer from latent *low* self-esteem in need of more elevating. Again, research does not support this "fact." Robyn Dawes wrote, "Hidden lack of self-esteem is the New Age psychologist's ether. A belief in undetected low self-esteem as a cause of undesirable behavior is even less plausible and all the available evidence directly contradicts it."[19]

Arrogant people don't suffer from parental failure to provide enough high self-esteem. The problem is that they were never taught to silence the self in favor of the family. They don't know how to function constructively within a system without focusing on manipulating it to their own personal advantage, and this family-thinking deficiency may be what ultimately leads them to think less of others. It is their unmet need to belong that is at the root of their selfish misconduct, not compensation for low self-esteem.

Parents don't need to worry as much as they do about nurturing their children's high self-esteem. They owe them the same thing their children owe them—loving, fair, patient, and honest feedback designed to promote the skill of intimate, caring connection. They owe them a loving place where they can fail, be told they've failed, and be told how to do better. They owe them the chance to grow up to be a practicing familist.

Familism Proposition Number Five: Children don't deserve a better life than their parents had.   As discussed earlier, another selfhelpism "parenting fact" is that we must strive to give our children a better life than we had, but this idea is deserving of more mindfulness. As parents, we should be leading our lives so that our children will want to lead theirs with the same integrity, purpose, and shared joy they see us experiencing.

If we seek to give our children more than we have, we are declaring our own lives to be less than they should be and can be. Is this a message we want to send our children? Do we want to convey to our children, even subtly, that we are discontent with our lot in life? Most children I've worked with in my clinic tell me how sad and worried it makes them feel when they think their parents aren't happy. Maybe we should spend more time learning how to share a savored life so that we can show our children how to do it. A little more demonstration of connective thriving and a little less emphasis on selfish striving would be good for the entire family. Maybe a little more "how to be family" and a little less emphasis on "how to be self-fulfilled" would help all of us.

Teaching the art of shared life savoring is more conducive to health and happiness than preaching about self-gratification. From my family's long hours by my bedside when I was ill, we've learned that one of the greatest gifts any of us can ever give our children is to show by our words and deeds that we ourselves are happy and privileged to be family, forever.

A Lively Livelihood

*The highest reward from your working is not
what you get for it but what you become by it.*

SYDNEY HARRIS

PROPOSITIONS ABOUT WORKING

1. Being a "workaholic" is good for your health.
2. An "unbalanced" life is a good one.
3. All our time is "quality time."
4. Time management is a waste of time.
5. Healthy success cannot be pursued.

WORKING TOWARD POVERTY

When Mother Teresa visited the United States, she described the slums of Calcutta as "the poorest place I've ever been in my life." She wasn't referring to economics. She was describing a general poverty of the soul, the condition I've been describing as mindlessness.

After he was diagnosed with a brain tumor, the successful Republican campaign strategist Lee Atwater said that confronting his own mortality had caused him to reconsider his view of success and how he had worked for it. He described how his cancer had awakened him to an awareness of the same "spiritual vacuum" in American society that Mother Teresa had observed. As he was dying, he described society's view of success as "a tumor of the soul." One source of this spiritual deficiency is our approach to work and how we have come to define success. Whether our livelihoods make us and those around us feel more alive or more drained of life's energy is a key issue in being able to savor our lives.

The authors John DeGraaf, David Wann, and Thomas Naylor refer to "affluenza," which they define as a socially transmitted condition of debt, anxiety, waste, disconnection, and endless work in the dogged pursuit of "more."[1] But do highly successful people really feel happy and fully alive?

TOXIC-SUCCESS SYNDROME

I have conducted twenty years of research on highly successful people and the way they approach work.[2] The state of mind Mother Teresa saw as a poverty of the soul and Lee Atwater called a "tumor of the soul" I called "toxic-success syndrome." It stems from the belief in a set of false facts about the nature of work, and self-help's definition of "the good life" and how it can be achieved. Even among those in my study who had attained the highest levels of success (measured by prestige and financial compensation), I discovered hundreds of languishing laborers who were too busy seeking happiness to find it squeezed somewhere between their noses and the grindstone.

My interviews indicated that Arnold Toynbee was right when he wrote that "the supreme accomplishment is to blur the line between work and play." When work is healthy, we feel alive, alert, and energized because we have worked well; when it is unhealthy, we are exhausted and distracted when it is finished.

More and more of us are working at home, and we think this will allow us more "living" time, but my research indicates that it doesn't. The home workers I studied at first believed they would be able to get up when they wanted, work in their pajamas, and have more "quality" time with their families. But that didn't happen. Most of them discovered that they still had to work in synchronization with the "work world" and became more and more sluggish by not having to "dress up"; they missed the socialization of the workplace, their family members grew tired of having them at home but not really "home," and family life was often disrupted by converting what should be a loving place into a workplace.

WIST-FULL

The psychologist Robert Emmons has studied how people work, live, and look for the happiness they seek. He refers to the "Big 4" elements of a meaningful, energizing life: Work, Intimacy, Spirituality, and Transcendence (WIST).[3] Like most researchers in the new science of positive psychology, Emmons has found that work is one of the key components of a positive life. However, work becomes just a job unless it has a vision beyond tangible rewards (intimacy), a sense of higher purpose in the work (spiritual peace), and a sense that working results in a connection with the world (transcendence).

My interviews indicated that most people spend more than half their waking hours at work and many more thinking about their work. Their ever-busy brains become so used to constant stimulation and "tasking" that any activity other than working—such as jogging, gardening, or even making love—is accompanied by constant stimulation to the brain by noise from headphones, computers, and televisions. At the gym, at family gatherings, or when retiring for the night, thoughts about work often crept into their consciousness.

We give our all to work, but we're failing to ask enough of it in return. Work should be one of the best ways to feel more alive and connected with others, but it's becoming increasingly a source of agitation. Despite all the technology that's supposed to make working more efficient, work demands more and more of our attention and time. If work was not going well, my subjects didn't feel well. They often said the words "family comes first," but it was work that was taking priority.

The self-help warning "never mix work and personal life" is not only impossible to heed—it's also the wrong advice. Our ways of loving and familying are inseparable from our ways of working. If it feels more like play than work, good work can make us and those who love us feel more alive and less dead tired. If you whistle more than sigh while you work, you probably have a pretty lively livelihood.

SPIRITUAL UNEMPLOYMENT

Eleanor Roosevelt once said, "When you cease to make a contribution you begin to die." Our young people are being denied the chance to make contributions. They are a generation practicing self-help to the max, yet they have very little opportunity to help themselves to a productive and contributing life. The more a family is able to provide for its children, the longer adulthood is postponed: The most privileged young people remain in a state of perpetual adolescence well into their twenties, and sometimes beyond. The underprivileged work at grinding, often unrewarding, jobs with little opportunity to further their education or realize their dreams, but those at the opposite end of the scale have turned the advantage of education into the chronic frustration of working to be successful rather than savoring success through doing one's work.

With compulsory education and the increasing value placed on independence and self-development, teenagers become more and more separated from adult life. They leave home and go to school, where their focus is largely on themselves and enhancing their self-esteem. They pay little attention to the benefits—social, spiritual, and practical—of working hard to achieve a goal located somewhere outside the self.

This perpetual adolescence is reflected in the self-help work ethos. Work is portrayed as simply another method by which we can "find ourselves," but healthy working stems from becoming more profoundly aware of others and the impact on them of what we do. The idea of contributing to society, of making the world a better place through industry, or of moving the focus off our selves and onto an abstract sense of higher purpose is a concept as foreign in the world of self-help as it is in most high schools and get-rich-quick infomercials.

THE PRIVILEGE OF DOING GOOD WORK

But the need to do contributing, meaningful work is real. The crisis of unemployment has major and wide-ranging practical consequences, but the pain goes deeper than financial stress and fears. Ask anyone who has been laid off and you will hear that feeling unemployed, or even underemployed, is also a crisis with spiritual proportions.

When cancer stopped me from working, I felt spiritually adrift and frustrated. I asked myself, "Why do so many people seem to be taking the privilege of being able to work for granted?" I promised myself that I would savor every moment of what I did for a living, and live so that those I loved could share that savoring with me.

Every day in my hospital room, I could hear symptoms of spiritual unemployment in the words of those who had high-paying and highly respected jobs. I listened as medical staff used terms such as "deskfast" (a hurried breakfast eaten at one's desk at work), "salmon day" (spending the day working hard but getting nowhere), and being a "stress puppy" (someone who complains about stress but secretly craves it). They spoke of "tasking," "multitasking," and "24/7" as facts of working life. I realized that their work had become primarily avenues for self-fulfillment rather than shared paths to a life well savored. That's when I coined the phrase "toxic success."

✌

During the many months of my hospitalization I was able to observe doctors, nurses, medical students, residents, cleaning men and women, and other hospital personnel doing their jobs. Although some of these people moaned and complained, it was often the people doing the more menial jobs in the hospital who took the most joy from working, savored what they were doing, and sanctified the tasks that constituted their work. They were the people the patients looked forward to seeing every day. They brought a zest to their work that was palpable even to people near death. As I watched more closely, I noticed that many if not most of those who savored their work were much less concerned with status or self-regard than with doing their jobs and seeing others being helped by what they were doing.

Physicians often approached their patients as if they were mechanics performing "procedures" on cars. They hurried through their rounds, scribbled in their medical charts, and moved on to the next task. They worked hard but not joyfully. When I asked one of them whether she was savoring being a doctor, she looked at me and laughed, "Oh, sure. As soon as I get a minute, I'll get right to savoring. Let me put that on my calendar right now."

ROSY THE HEALER

Then there was Rosy. Like many of the women and men who regularly cleaned and mopped my room, she loved what she was doing and usually whistled while she worked. I can't remember seeing my doctors humming or singing, but Rosy almost always did. Rosy was a nurse's aide, which meant she did a lot of dirty work for little pay. She cleaned us when we vomited, wiped us when we could not control our bowels, and dumped and measured our urine output. Despite this difficult work, Rosy always had a blast and brought a sense of liveliness to a place so permeated with the sense of death.

I have never found a better example of someone who performed unselfish savored work than Rosy. She said she had never read "one of those help-yourself books," but I wish she would write one. I learned later that Rosy was happily married and valued her family as the center of her life. She was elevated by the simplest tasks related to her job. She was totally authentic in her feelings about her work and her interactions with the patients and staff. She was a model of humility, always appreciative of her opportunity to work, and forgiving, or at least tolerant, of the most obnoxious patient or staff member. Perhaps most of all, she was mindful of her mission and her commitment to the welfare of her patients.

Rosy spoke with pride about being employed by the hospital. She was fiercely loyal to the staff, to the patients, and to the mission of healing. She would always smile, say hello, and narrate her tasks as if she were doing delicate surgery in front of a theater of medical students. She would pause at the end of her work and earnestly scan the room for anything she might have missed.

Rosy always referred to herself in the third person (I came to think of this as a small rebellion against a relentlessly "I"-focused society). As if she had literally lost herself in her work, when it was done, she would always ask, "Is there anything else Rosy can do for you before she leaves?" If nothing was requested, she would bow her head and remain silent for just a moment, and then say in a very low whisper, "God bless you. See you tomorrow."

When I was being discharged from the hospital, I wanted to say goodbye to Rosy because she had been crucial to my healing. I found her working on another floor in the hospital. I could hear her singing, and when she saw me, she threw down her mop, spread open her arms, and ran to me. She stopped suddenly and said, "Oh, oh. Is it O.K. for Rosy to give you a big hug now? She couldn't hug you on the transplant unit. Is it safe now?"

"I'm sorry," I said, "the doctors say no." I was still wearing a surgical mask and it was wet with my tears. "O.K.," she said, "then here's a long-distance hug, care of Rosy." She smiled, wrapped her arms around a pile of bed sheets, and laughed. I asked whether I could speak with her for just a few moments alone. As we sat on opposite ends of a long bench, I asked her why she loved her work so much. She answered, "It really feels more like play. It's Rosy's calling. If she don't do what she do, everything the docs and nurses do might not work. Rosy's a healer in her own way, and she loves doing it." I asked why she always stood silently before she left my room and her answer reflected the spirituality with which she approached her calling. For the first time, I saw embarrassment on Rosy's face. She looked around, looked down, and whispered in the same soft voice she always used just before she left my room: "Rosy always says a little prayer in each room for every patient. It slows her down, but she don't care about the clock. It's just a way Rosy has of ending her little healing ceremonies in each room. Rosy was called to heal people, and this is how she does it." She laughed and slapped her thigh, saying, "There, you see? You thought Rosy was just a nurse's aide, but she's really a healer disguised as a nurse's aide."

PSYCHOLOGICAL ABSENTEEISM

Because there can be no consumption without production, most people have to work to make a living. Unfortunately, this need often limits our work by turning it into a job to get done or a career to be pursued, but not the kind of response to a calling that Rosy showed every day.

Research shows that there are two sources of reward for our working, extrinsic and intrinsic. Extrinsic reward is financial—related to perks, privileges, and status. Intrinsic rewards are what Rosy received, a sense of accomplishment by doing valued and essential work for the common good. In an increasingly hectic workplace characterized by electronic connections instead of personal contact, short-term employment instead of long-term commitment, and a considerable gap between what one does every day and the final product or service the public actually experiences, extrinsic rewards have become dominant. Even if we do love our work and say we would do it for no pay, high rewards can actually rob that work of its intrinsic value. The result is a job or career rather than a calling.

It's not dissatisfaction that is causing our failure to savor work. It's that we are psychologically absent, mindlessly going about our hectic days without paying attention to what we are doing or, which is more important, why and for whom we're doing it. We evaluate and are evaluated, but that's not being mindful. Our minds are at home when we're at work and at work when we're at home. We are seldom fully anywhere; instead, like adolescents, we're always getting ready to do, to go, or to be something else.

24/7, 8/5, and Stress-Induced Stress

Because so many workers feel stressed, hurried, and pressured to work "24/7," I seldom meet anyone who remembered "8=5," working eight hours a day five days a week. The fulfillment of potential requires what we think is constant timesaving, but in effect, we are wasting our lives. We have become a nation of compulsive clock-watchers, and personal power over time is a major objective. I don't understand what we're doing with all the time we are allegedly saving, because no one ever has enough of it.

When Cream of Wheat was introduced in 1893, it was touted as "instant breakfast" because it took only fifteen minutes to prepare. By 1939, the time was down to five minutes, and today it takes thirty seconds. In the early 1800s, Beethoven's concerts ran more than six hours.

In the mid-1980s, the standard classical music concert was two hours long. Now audience members fidget if the performance approaches ninety minutes. Home cooking, walking, reading, conversation, and writing letters have been replaced by fast food, driving, the Web, instant messages, and e-mail.[4] Even One-Hour-Photo isn't fast enough—digital is "instant." All this acceleration has become accepted as normal. Self-help experts are invited by corporations to help their employees learn "time management," but *attention* management is the real problem.

Workers and their employers know that rushed, unhappy, and un-healthy people result in unhealthy organizations and a suffering bottom line. To deal with this problem, a set of false facts—again, based on self-helpism—emerged in what has become a largely failed attempt at "stress management."

The cure for our hurry and stress is sought by even more "doing." One person told me, "As if I don't already have enough stress in my life, now I have the stress of trying to reduce stress. I'm suffering from stress-induced stress."

Like someone who regularly takes antacids without asking himself why he keeps eating such indigestible food, we decide to accept and then try to manage our stress. Because "everyone is doing it," the silent epidemic of languishing and the soul-numbing speed that contributes to it are accepted as "normal." This kind of ever-accelerating normalcy is a major threat to our health, and that is particularly true when it comes to how we work.

THE BLISS AND BENEFITS OF BEING TYPE A

Being "Type A" has become such a popular concept that people now either brag about being guilty of it or admit to it with the same help-less surrender of someone who eats too much junk food. Being hard-working, competitive, totally into our work, full of energy, always on the go, eager to get to work, time-pressured, and working long hours are often identified as the symptoms of being a "Type A" personality. These traits are not a risk to our health and they may even be good for it. According to the neuroscientist Robert Sapolsky, "Being time-pressured, impatient, and overachieving probably has little to do with heart disease risk."[5]

Type A is the perfect self-help concept. It is intuitively right, and taps into our sense that we are not realizing our full self-potential. Like the "addictive personality," it affords us victim status and the emotional cover that we are suffering from a documented disease. "Type A" has become a kind of potentialism disease, a "hurry sickness."

That haste lays waste to our coronary arteries may appear to be only common sense, but it remains unproven. In fact, more than three decades of research have failed to provide proof that hard work and feeling pressured by time kills us. It turns out that it is not going fast and working hard but thinking fast and being selfishly hostile that can kill us.

Type A was proposed in 1959 by the cardiologists Meyer Friedman and Ray Rosenman as a "harrying sense of time urgency."[6] Like many of self-helpism's "facts," the idea of Type A is what the author James Gleick calls "a notion with no particular scientific validity."[7] The original research on Type A was on a small group of eighty-three men, a group labeled "Group A." It was made up of successful businessmen who weighed more, drank more, and smoked more than the members of the control group, "Group B." Group B was never fully studied and was used primarily as a foil against which to compare the cardio-cursed Type A's.

I elaborate on the false fact of Type A because it shows how poorly conducted science can turn an idea into accepted fact. Type A's evolution from opinion to fact is like many self-help principles that become self-fulfilling prophecies. So-called Type A's are running around every-where in fine health and are often healthier than the more lethargic Type B's, whom they constantly aggravate.

When I mindfully thought about the Type A idea and checked the research, I discovered it is not the powerful explanatory concept we thought it was. If Type A's do represent a danger, it's that their failure to share a savored life can annoy the heck out of the calmer Type B's they live with.

A closer look at "Type A" and the research about it shows that the "combat readiness" mind-set of some people is the real health risk, not being time-pressured, competitive, or hurried.[8] Some people when challenged react "hot." Even a confronting word or perceived attack can cause the defensive reacting and agitated nervous system to kick in. The body prepares in milliseconds for war. Blood is diverted to the muscles so they can pack a stronger punch. Taken from the internal organs such as the liver, the diverted blood isn't filtered of toxic substances; these substances are then more likely to deposit themselves in the arteries around the heart.

The heart can begin to beat irregularly almost as if it's trembling in anticipation of attack. One might experience atrial fibrillation, meaning that the two upper chambers of the heart contract too fast. Over time, the muscles of the heart chambers become firmer and harder. We may want to have buns of steel, but not a heart of steel. A hard heart eventually fails.

Here are some of self-help's lessons about how we are supposed to manage work stress. I took each of them from presentations by motivational speakers presenting for large corporate meetings, and from time-management self-help books:

- Don't be Type A. It can kill you.
- Cut back!
- Learn to manage your time.
- It's not the quantity of the time you spend with your family, it's the quality of that time.
- Don't be a "workaholic."

- Live your life in balance.
- Practice "stress-reduction" techniques.
- Multitasking saves time.
- Don't bring your work problems home.
- Be unconditionally supportive to your stressed spouse.

Audiences love to hear these words of wisdom about stress and work. They appear in many forms in popular books about how to balance working and family life, but I've learned that, like all the self-help bromides you've been reading about, they require a lot more mindfulness than we've been giving them.

Five Propositions About Working

Here are the ideas about work and daily stress that I've come up with. They are based on my own toxic-success study and the most current research about healthy working. I invite you to put your mind to them before you begin your next time-management or stress-reduction program.

Working Proposition Number One: Being a "workaholic" is good for your health. One of the many false addictions advocated by self-helpism is "workaholism." Supposedly suffering from the hurry and haste disease, workaholics are thought to represent the compulsive extreme of Type A. Again, this assertion is without scientific merit and another phony self-help "alohaism."

According to the psychologist Marilyn Machlowitz, a workaholic is "a blur of a person rushing by with an overflowing briefcase, dictating into a tape recorder, checking the time, and munching on a sandwich."[9] That may be how some people work and live, but no one becomes addicted to this behavior or goes into physical withdrawal when they stop. They may love their work so much that they never want to stop, but thinking of them as addicts explains nothing and diminishes the gravity of true addiction.

What is missing from the idea of Type A and workaholism is the sense of connection with others. Again, self-helpism sees most problems as existing "within" the damaged self rather than "between" selves. Someone who loves working in a blur of activity is likely to be uncomfortable living with someone who prefers blissful peace and quiet.

The person who sees a mountain and must climb it "because it is there" isn't going to be happy for long with someone who sees a mountain and has to sit down and rest against it just "because it is there." Self-helpism sees work and its associated daily stress as it does other areas of life, that is, from the perspective of the individual rather than from a shared perspective. It ignores the truth that if the people who love us live and work in the same way we do, being a workaholic can be good not only for our health but also for our relationship's health.

Almost every one of the self-labeled "workaholics" in my toxic-success study said they loved their work, that it was more like playing than working, that they felt more alive when they were doing it. Again, what matters most about working is how our behavior impacts those around us. Some of us have a hard-work temperament and others don't. If you marry someone who shares or at least understands the "work is my fun" orientation, your health is more likely to be enhanced than if you try to calm down, cut back, and be what you are not. There is no evidence that hard, long, vigorous, fully involved, and enjoyed work is dangerous to the health, but there's plenty of research to show that constant striving to be who we're not can kill us.

Working Proposition Number Two: An "unbalanced" life is a good one.   Is your life in balance? I hope not. Perfect balance is not only an unattainable goal, but we would be huge bores if it we could attain it. There's no precedence for balance anywhere in nature. Forests, oceans, and the stars are in a constant state of flux. A forest may look as if it's in perfect peaceful balance, but it's teeming with life and death.

When I was ill, I longed to be immersed again in life's natural chaos and adversities. I always knew I was in for more suffering and on the verge of another problem when things appeared to be getting "back into balance." What I thought was an indication that things were improving usually turned out to be a dangerous sign of stagnation. The natural and healthy state of life is *imbalance*, not balance. The healthiest heart rhythm is one that is chaotic and varied. Blood pressure that never changes is a sign that something might be wrong. We are naturally un-balanced participants in a constantly chaotic world. Struggling to live in balance is as impossible as standing perfectly still. In other words, as beautiful and magnificent as life can sometimes be, the calm times within it are always states of transition. Beneath the surface of bliss, there is always the hum of nature's infinite upheaval.

Healthy working is not finding balance in our lives. In many ways, it's looking for and trying to create more imbalance by coming up with new ideas, approaches, and challenges. Healthy working is joining with the people who matter most to celebrate temporary victories and to grow stronger through life's traumas. I call this "shared catastrophe contentedness," and it's the lesson we cancer patients learned: Life in perfect balance is not only impossible and undesirable, it's also a dan-ger sign.

The South African author Sir Laurens van der Post wrote of his en-counter with Carl Jung: "[He] told me with a laugh that he could not imagine a fate more awful, a fate worse than death, than a life lived in perfect harmony and balance."[10] If you feel you are working too hard, under too much stress, don't have enough time, and if your life is in chaos, enjoy it. Again, that's life. Start savoring it. Focus less on saving time than savoring the time you have. Worry less about balance and start enjoying the perfect mess you are in.

Working Proposition Number Three: All our time is "quality time." My central thesis in this book has been that the quality of life is largely determined by a willingness to be mindful and to control the content of our consciousness. If this is true, what becomes "quality time" depends on where and how we focus our attention and decide what we will put *on* our minds. Time has quality when we mindfully attend to all the moments that become what we have made of the gift of life.

Self-help programs are fond of dividing time into categories such as "healing time," "personal space time," and "tasking time," but mindful savoring of life involves a much less compartmentalized view of time. Just as we have "a" life and not sex lives, work lives, love lives, and parenting lives, we delude ourselves when we think we are somehow different and think and act in different ways at different times. We do "bring our work problems home" because we *are* the problem.

By cordoning off a few hours of the week as "quality time," we see the rest of our time as of lesser value, not worth attention. After coming so close to running out of time myself, I've learned to be more mindful of *all* my moments, even the simplest. I love brushing my teeth, drinking water, and just sitting around doing nothing. I do my best to make whatever time I have less mindless and more sacred.

Working Proposition Number Four: Time management is a waste of time.   Speaking of time, until we learn to manage our attention, all the self-helpism time-management programs in the world will be useless. Since the 1960s, hundreds of books have suggested ways to manage time as if it were a limited resource. Experts on organization forget that time is not money, and that it can only be spent, not saved. In fact, in many ways, time doesn't exist at all. It's another one of our inventions used to provide some sense of control and to help us structure our lives, but it is not real. Time may not be on our side, but it is in our minds. We'll never "have a moment" if we don't take it.

Time has gone from being an invention of convenience to the dictator of our lives. When I ask my patients to not wear a watch, they vehemently resist. "Get real," they say, but our capacity to place our attention where we choose is what is real. A huge amount of attention can be given to someone or something in a very short period of clock time. I remember when I was at a stoplight: Our car windows were down and I heard the lady in the next car sneeze. I smiled and said, "God bless you." She smiled back and said, "Thanks." For me, that brief moment in time was sanctified by a simple act of interpersonal acknowledgement.

"Flow" is one of the savoring arts. Research into it shows that it derives from doing something so engaging that we lose all sense of time and of ourselves.[11] We don't evaluate, we luxuriate in the present moment and task at hand. The opposite of work stress, flow is a feeling of being so into what we are doing that ideas such as reward, power, and prestige lose their meaning.

Instead of attending time-management seminars, we need to go home and pay more attention to the people who matter most. Attention is not only the new business currency, it's the currency of love. We must find a way to work that doesn't just enhance our sense of self but causes it to disappear completely. We need to find work that allows us time to take back our greatest human gift: our capacity to control our attention.

Working Proposition Number Five: Healthy success cannot be pursued.

Tap into your personal power! Set high goals and go for them! Quitters never win and winners never quit! You only fail if you think you will! Don't just compete: crush your competitor! Know the thrill of victory and never experience the agony of defeat. If you think you can, you will, but if you think you can't, you won't. You can have it! It all comes down to a matter of willpower. Nobody remembers who came in second. Success, ladies and gentlemen, is yours for the taking, but first you have to really, really want it! Do you want it? I can't hear you! Do you really, really want it?

These were the exact words of a motivational speaker addressing one of the largest insurance companies in the world. The motivationalist's speech was like a pep rally. He was addressing five hundred of the company's top sales people. They cheered in response to every self-help phrase and rose to their feet even before he had finished. He exited the stage to the theme of the movie *Rocky*; behind him were two large screens showing violent football tackles. Audience members reached out to try to touch him as he left the room.

This was self-help theater at its very best. It contained several of its facts of life, including personal power, awakened inner giants, self-actualization, the happiness ethic, self-love, and mind over matter. The speaker's central point was that success is simply a matter of wanting it—and selfishly pursuing it at all costs. Watching the audience's reaction depressed me. I thought, "Why aren't they asking 'How do you know?' Why do they accept this pop psychology self-helpism so willingly?" Then I remembered H. G. Wells's story about Tono-Bungay and the gullible masses searching for answers, willing to put their trust in authoritative pronouncements presented with marketing savvy. I thought about my own study of toxic success and how so many successful men and women were languishing, or mistaking an intense personal life for a shared meaningful one.

I have come to believe that, contrary to self-help's mantra of personal power, success cannot be pursued in a healthy way. Success, as it is defined in today's work world, means the accumulation of money, power, and prestige. When all our attention is focused on this goal, we risk ignoring the very things that make life worth living—that lead to real success. Our families, our spiritual selves, our connection with a community, our sense of peace, our sense of lively engagement in life and with others, all these vital elements of a good life are cast aside in the relentless, self-defeating pursuit of personal success.

It's hardly radical to say that the happiest people are those who find joy in all elements of their lives, and that the most "successful" people, those with the most toys, are often miserable and alone. Yet still we persist in looking for a way to pursue success in a "healthy" way. To me, this is akin to smoking "additive-free" cigarettes. If you're concerned about the terrible effects smoking has on your body, *give up smoking*. If you're worried about the toxic impact that the pursuit of success is having on your life, *give up the chase*. Reevaluate your values. Redefine success. Find a job where you can whistle while you work.

Ultimately, success of any kind cannot be experienced individually. It happens when we are less selfish, more attentive to what (and who) matters most in life, and no longer accept that our victories necessitate someone else's defeat. It comes when we no longer mistake intensity for meaning, and the transient pleasure of what we get for the infinite joy of what we give.

Escape from Health Hysteria

Health is not a matter of doing. It is a matter of being.

ABRAHAM MASLOW

PROPOSITIONS ABOUT HEALTH AND HEALING

1. Illness is essential to your health.
2. Indulgence is good.
3. There is no such thing as an illness-causing emotion.
4. A positive attitude is not necessary for healing.
5. Giving up is essential to healing

HOW ARE YOU?

The best answer to that most common question might be "Compared to what?" How we answer reflects our view of what we consider to be a healthy life. If we answer "Great" or "Fine," we are often just exchanging social graces instead of delivering a lengthy review of our overall health. Some of us answer according to the absence of symptoms: "Not bad," or "I'm hanging in there." One of my friends answered by joking, "Able to sit up and take nourishment." The common answer of "Okay" indicates that we settled for the idea that health is the absence of sickness and the slowest rate at which we can die.

If we pause a few moments to reflect mindfully on the question "How are you?" we come to realize that it is a complex and fundamental inquiry into how we are leading our lives. It's a kind of "health dipstick" that reveals our definition of day-to-day well-being compared to that of others we know. When self-helpism establishes health goals we can't attain, we stop trying to attain them and become a society of diet dropouts holding unused and expired health club passes.

We've become a society of the worried well, held hostage by a modern health hysteria that's constantly warning us about our vulnerabilities and nagging us about our failures to comply with the latest program. This pathogenic orientation often ignores our natural resilience and capacity to thrive in the most difficult times. We are warned that nearly everything we enjoy can kill us. As a result, we end up practicing sickness self-defense rather than truly savoring our daily living.

The word *health* derives from an old German word represented in the English language by the words *hale* and *whole*. Linguists trace these two words back to the medieval battlefield and the loss of *haleness* to severe injury, but our health is not limited to the absence of sword wounds inflicted by "the daily wars" of modern living.[1]

The World Health Organization, in its 1946 charter, defined health as "a state of complete physical, mental, and social well-being and not merely the absence of disease or infirmity." That certainly sounds like a worthy goal, but can anyone ever be in a state of *complete* health? I suggest that this is an impossible goal and that pursuing it is another example of self-helpism's blind passion for totally fulfilled personal potential.

∽

There's an ancient cemetery outside the Cathedral Necropolis in Scotland that may hold a forgotten secret of health. In the early 1990s, researcher George Davey Smith conducted a study that asked a creative and strange question: Could the grave markers at the old cemetery hold any information about the health and longevity of the deceased?[2] To answer this question, he compared the height of each grave marker to the age of the person buried beneath it at the time of death. What he discovered points out the error of assuming that good health is a matter of genetic good luck, a Spartan diet, running like a hamster on a treadmill, pleasure-denying willpower, and practicing the latest "self-health" approach.

Smith found that the taller the grave marker, the longer the life. The deceased men with tall obelisks had lived on average three years longer than those with shorter markers, and the same test held true for the women. Of course, buying yourself a tall gravestone now won't make you live longer. Smith was looking for correlations between the affluence that allowed such a purchase and health and longevity; what he found is one of the most clearly established (but usually ignored) health factors, what scientists now call the SEP factor: *socioeconomic position*.

The three major components of SEP are income, education, and occupational status, none of which are accounted for in most self-help programs. Based on current research, creative self-help regarding our health might be facilitated if doctors would not just take blood pressure but also ask how we feel about what we earn, if we feel that we're continuing to learn, and how proud we are about what we do for a living.

Smith discovered that the grave markers had been an important indicator of social prestige and wealth. The richer the person, the taller the marker. Then, as now, affluent people tended to be healthier and to live longer than poor people.[3]

Does the SEP effect simply tell us what we already know: that rich people live in safer and better neighborhoods, eat healthier food, and have access to better health care than the poor? Well, yes—but there's more. Although we don't have all the answers to why rich people live longer, studies of differences between the well-to-do and the impoverished indicate that how we *feel* about where we are on the social ladder matters a great deal, and it's not just the gap between the really rich and the terribly poor that's involved here. We all compare ourselves with others on the three SEP factors, and that comparison is an important and often forgotten dimension of health.

We mislead ourselves if we think we can easily change our health by adopting a certain attitude or by eating the right food. Our health exists within a system. How we behave, how we feel, and how we see ourselves within that system are often-overlooked "steps" in self-help programs.

THE GREAT DIET SCAM

Despite a dieting industry worth $40 billion, most of the wealthiest people in the world are still too fat. Despite the equally lucrative exercise equipment and health club industry that promises a new body in just months, most Americans are still out of shape.

Constant reminders that we're too fat, we eat the wrong things, and we don't exercise enough may cause just enough guilt and fear to persuade us to buy diet books and treadmills, but not enough to make us use them consistently. Change is easy, but staying changed isn't. Without a mindful approach to enjoying the health we already have and what we want to change about our health, we end up feeling as though we're killing ourselves in our stressful efforts to stay healthy and reduce stress.

Self-help explains our failure to stay changed by declaring that we have not yet realized our human potential for self-control, we don't understand the nature of an addictive personality, and we don't know how to think positively. Self-help diagnoses us as being addicted to the wrong food and to watching television.

The diet gurus think that our incessant nibbling will eventually be controlled by their bombardment of silly sound bites: "Weight control begins with finger control," "Change your mind and you will change your meal," "Those who think thin become thin." This kind of oversimplification merely adds to the problem. *If it's as easy as thinking thin,* you might reasonably ask yourself, *am I just a fat head?* The diet craze has caused millions of Americans to feel like health reprobates lacking the personal power to "stick with" whatever latest guaranteed program they've been sold. Most research shows that body weight is strongly influenced by genetics. Even though most popular diets work for a little while, they have little scientific proof of long-term healthy weight regulation. We lose more money than weight on fad diets, and the recent fading of the "no carbs" approach to "fewer carbs" is evidence of the diet roulette on which so many gamble their health and happiness.

Aztec Medicine

When chemotherapy had deadened my taste buds, for some strange reason I maintained my sweet tooth. I craved chocolate, but my doctors warned that it was "junk food" and that I should avoid it at all costs. I defied their advice, telling them that the Aztecs considered chocolate a gift from the gods and so did I. Amid the bitterness of medicines and chemotherapy, I had no intention of denying myself the chance to savor the sweet taste of chocolate. I felt a little healthier whenever I indulged myself in this unhealthy pleasure.

Modern medicine is often guilty of the same unmindful assumptions that characterize self-helpism. But science is never black and white, as my chocolate example demonstrates. We are repeatedly cautioned that chocolate is fattening and leads to clogged arteries and rotten teeth. Yet research shows that, at least in my case, something that tastes good, smells good, and looks good can also *be* good for us. Dark chocolate in particular contains plant substances calls polyphenols, the same components that give red wine some of its heart-healthy attributes.[4] As for the warnings about decaying teeth, chocolate actually contains substances that help protect tooth enamel.[5] I am not suggesting that we manage heart disease, hypertension, and tooth decay with the motto "a chocolate bar a day keeps the doctor away," but I am suggesting that a thriving state of health is more a matter of moderation than of martyrdom.

Most Risk Factors Aren't As Risky As You Think

I know of a young man who found his algebra class utterly mystifying. He told his mother, "One day they'll say X equals five—and the next day they'll say it equals seventeen!" I must admit, I feel the same way about "risk factors" as he did about algebraic factors. The statistics given today might not be the same tomorrow, and new ones are always coming.

Half the people who suffer heart attacks have none of the well-known risk factors such as smoking and obesity. Half of those who *do* have these risk factors never have a heart attack.[6] Most of us know or have heard of people who avoided every risk factor but still died young, and of others who were health reprobates yet lived to ripe old ages.

A study of several hundred men in their seventies has been conducted by the University of Hawaii.[7] As a perfect example of the contrary consciousness I'm encouraging, the study showed that those with the lowest cholesterol actually had a *higher* risk of heart attack or stroke. Studies on the benefits of exercise constantly contradict one another about how much is enough to stay healthy.

To stave off death, millions now deny themselves many of the simple pleasures of life. Indulgence, which really only means "to gratify or satisfy a desire," has earned an undeserved bad name, particularly among those who think their self-potential requires them to have buns of steel and abs that ripple. When all their sacrifices and avoidance of simple indulgences fail to give them the body or health they covet, they turn to alternatives.

∽

For those unhappy with the pessimistic orientation of modern medicine, "alternative medicine" has emerged as the panacea to our dissatisfaction with allopathic medicine. Alternative medicine has become a denomination within the religion of self-helpism, and thousands have turned to it.

Alternative medicine approaches are derived from various combinations of Japanese, Indian ayurvedic, Chinese, Native American, and other ancient medical or shamanistic systems. The various practices are usually taught by psychologists, layperson gurus, and, less frequently, by self-help born-again physicians who have broken away from their pathogenic and mechanical medical training. Alternative medicine has its roots in ancient healing systems, but unfortunately, many modern alternative medicine practitioners try to apply the techniques of these systems without understanding and respecting their ancestral and cultural roots. These practitioners make the ancient systems "their own" and lose sight of the origins and the long-developed wisdom of the ancient people who created them. The result of cultural blindness to alternative medicine has been a plethora of practices, techniques, and programs that can be as spiritually and scientifically deprived as any of the modern medicinal specialties.

I have watched sadly as several people I know abandoned modern medicine and, with unshaken trust in "holistic" medicine or their guru's advice, slowly sickened and died. Modern medicine is far from perfect and does more than its share of damage, but it is also immensely powerful in what it can do. I don't know whether those who turned exclusively to alternative medicines would have lived had they followed the often toxic and invasive approaches of modern oncology. But I question what was really "holistic" about their decision when they denied themselves access to modern medicine.

"Holistic" does not mean desperately trying any alternative that might work; it means researching the evidence about what has worked for others in the past, including modern medical research and practice as well as ancient cultural wisdom. I suggest that we are more likely to be helped by one carefully mindful and research-based inclusive medicine than the current health hodge-podge alternative approaches.

PERPETUAL PATIENTS

The role of the healer can be traced back at least 17,000 years. That's the age of a cave painting discovered in southern France that depicts an Ice Age shaman wearing the animal mask of a witch doctor. Exactly when the idea of *self*-healing got started is harder to determine, but the human-potential movement gained momentum in the early 1960s. The question of whether we can heal ourselves is worthy of mindful consideration for practicing creative self-help.

The philosopher Josiah Royce wrote, "Whoever, in his own mind, makes the whole great world center about the fact that he, just this private individual, once was ill and now is well, is still a patient."[8] Self-helpism's relentless focus on personal recovery from an assumed illness or addiction—indeed, its insistence that we draw an identity from that recovery—bears this out. Remember, if we weren't perpetual patients, always recovering but never recovered, self-help would go bust.

As you have read, the self-help movement assumes that something is wrong with the self; what's wrong is isolated in the individual and not in her connections, and the patient herself is the ultimate healer. It teaches that the best way to deal with adversity is to tap into our inner resources and develop a positive attitude. But my experience with healing suggests that the contrary is true. Although taking personal charge of one's health can be helpful, I found that giving up and connecting dependently with others was at least as essential to healing; in this way, I came to view self-help as too selfish to be of help when the chips are down.

The popular notion of one mind trying to exert itself over matter is insufficient for healing, which is a difficult and sacred human process.

Healing is a reconnective process involving *shared* consciousness (rather than increased *self*-consciousness) and an increased awareness of where we fit into the world around us.

Sickness is caused by and results in real or imagined separation. The more self-help we try, the more detached we can become. The popular concepts of imagery and visualization are private endeavors that have their place, but when I was sick, I wanted more than anything else to do things with people, not be trapped in my own "inner self." Even the idea of "self-healing" made me feel isolated and afraid.

The patient's frame of mind can be lonely and self-focused, but healing requires *collective* thinking at least as much as positive thinking. Healing can be enhanced by turning focus outside the self. Try listening to others, asking about their pains and fears, touching and massaging loved ones rather than always being the "touchee"; in this sense, healing is a process of more mindfully engaging in the world with others. The next time you're sick or hospitalized, immediately send flowers to someone else.

Into the Gray Area

Shlomo Breznitz wrote about the existence between life and death that many of us who have faced our own or a loved one's mortality know all too well. He said, "It is in the gray area between the possible and futile that the battle of coping with stress has to be fought."[9] Gray well defines the color of my life when cancer began to deplete the energy of my soul as well as my body. It's the color of a soul that not only tires of the struggle but begins to doubt its worth.

When a terrible crisis strikes, you are thrust into a new realm. When you are told that your own death is approaching or that someone you love has died, the world—sometimes even literally—dims. Many people in these circumstances report living in a gray area—somewhere between trying to stay alive and the dangerous appeal of allowing life to fade away. When life is cruel, it can be painful to be mindful. That's when simplistic self-help techniques can be so seductively appealing. They give us something "to do" when nothing else works.

I once saw a "Do Not Disturb: Healing in Progress" sign on the door of one of my fellow patients' hospital room. I peeked in to see her sitting in the chair next to her bed staring off into space and muttering to herself. She later told me she was doing her daily "self-healing positive affirmations." I know there are times when being alone can be necessary and restful, but I made my own sign. It said, "Please Disturb. Help Wanted for Healing." I felt I had a mind of my own and that it was often letting me down. What I needed was someone else to join with me to reflect mindfully on what was happening to me and to help put it in a connective healing context.

∽

Healing involves various combinations of strengths, including fighting, growing, and sometimes just giving up. It is sometimes easier to struggle to survive life's traumas than to heal through quitting and moving on to different challenges. In today's "personal power" climate, everyone loves fighters and encourages them, but no one respects a quitter. So mindful surrender is one of the most difficult of healing challenges.

Survival is life's longing for itself, a kind of built-in evolutionary default mode. Fighting to survive comes naturally as a means to keep us going against all odds. The drive to survive is automatic and will take care of itself. We don't have to buy a self-help book to do it. But healing also requires that we thrive *because* of a crisis, which is not so instinctual. Thriving is more difficult than surviving because it requires that we know when we are wasting valuable creative energy.

Being a creative quitter is a difficult but powerful healing act. It means giving up when we know we must and then growing in new ways we never imagined we could. Healing involves looking at *all* our mental options to find a way through, including giving up and looking for new options. I found my own path to healing much less a "battle against cancer" than a mindful exploration of new ways to be more engaged in my current life with others.

"Giving up" has a bad reputation, but sometimes quitters do win. Healers know when it is time to disengage from a challenge, to set new goals, or to give up setting goals entirely for a while. Sometimes perseverance is only stubborn stupidity, and giving up can turn out to be the most intelligent and graceful response to adversity.

～

In my book *The Beethoven Factor*, I referred to the great composer's ability to write his *Ode to Joy* when he was deaf and dying.[10] I picked Beethoven as my role model for healing through adversity because he was a flawed man—far from the ideal of the self-help movement. He sulked, he complained, he got jealous; he gave up, he grew angry, and he was often an emotional mess. Beethoven the man was never cured, but his music shows that his genius continued to grow *because* of his suffering, not in spite of it.

Beethoven continued to suffer to the end of his life. But through it all, he chose creativity over reactivity and remained connected with his music even when physical reality stood in the way. He was far from a strong-willed fighter, but he remained in charge of how he would perceive his situation, gave up on his goals for marriage and the life he had long planned, and moved on to connect with music in new and unique ways. He penned different, extraordinarily creative music that inspires and soothes listeners throughout the world even today. The string quartets he composed as he was dying represented an entirely new approach to composition that were as much evidence of spiritual surrender as of strong character.

Beethoven's life was not characterized by the loving interpersonal connection that can be another key component of healing, but his music offered him a means to connect with the world even as he was physically shut off from so much of it. He connected with the past by looking for inspiration from past authors, poets, and composers. He connected with the future through his legacy of remarkable music. And through his gifts, he continues to promote connection and the promise of creative healing through his timeless compositions. He gave up one way of composing that was dependent on skills he no longer had, but he found new and ingenious ways to become whole again that may have been unavailable to him had he refused to give up and move on.

ARE WE ALL CRAZY?

Although I have been focusing primarily on healing as related to physical illness, mental illness offers its own devastating brand of suffering and need for healing. It is profoundly disconnecting and alienating. It creates major obstacles to being able to savor our lives and can tear at the very soul of the family.

According to self-helpism and the field of psychology, we are all growing mentally sicker. The bible of dysfunction, the *Diagnostic and Statistical Manual of Mental Disorders*, has grown from eighty-six pages in 1952 to almost nine hundred in 1994. The number of mental disorders has increased from 106 to 297 and counting. But this is not an accurate picture of how to establish mental health. If everything we think, feel, do, or desire that is not perfectly logical or adaptive is labeled as mentally ill, then mental health itself becomes so rare that it is the ultimate abnormal condition.

It is important to remember that what we now diagnose as disease and emotional or mental dysfunction were not always there, waiting to be discovered. They are categories created by a sickness-oriented health-care system and they are as much opinion as fact. Healing requires looking beyond labels and diagnosis to considering how we are relating with the world. If we look long enough and think slowly enough about life, we usually discover that there is much more that is right with us than is wrong.

Unless the latest medical warning or a new self-help program has convinced us otherwise, most of us—if we put our minds to it—will see that we are doing pretty well most of the time. Think about it: When you're feeling down, don't you eventually get better with no outside help or intentional effort at self-healing at all? Whatever "it" was, "it" just goes away. That's why one of the first and best things to do when we think we're sick is nothing.

Even when the problem is bigger than a blue day, our minds are amazingly resilient. Research shows that during their lives most people are exposed to at least one violent or life-threatening situation.[11] Although self-help approaches abound, most of us manage to thrive through the crisis without counseling, therapy, or a self-help program.

The psychologist George A. Bonanno has researched the phenomena of thriving through adversity and emotional healing at times of major loss. He points out that the traditional psychological approach to trauma is to offer help in the form of "grief work," or guiding patients through a process of "working through" suffering. His research challenges this model and shows that we may not be in need of as much help as we are being offered. Bonanno wrote, "Large numbers of people manage to endure the temporary upheaval of loss or potentially traumatic events remarkably well, with no apparent disruption in their ability to function at work or in close relationships, and seem to move on to new challenges with apparent ease."[12]

∽

According the current medical diagnostic criteria, three out of four of us are sick.[13] Like self-helpism, modern medicine looks for trouble and usually finds it. One physician has suggested that eventually every well person will be labeled sick: "As with the extinction of any species, there will be one last survivor" who will be "the last well person."[14]

Why are the citizens of the wealthiest country in the world so sick—and so worried about being sick? One reason is that we think about ourselves too much. We sense on some level that our unmindful daily lives are not healthy, and we fear the inevitable consequences. When we do take the time to be more mindful about life, we become more fully conscious of just how toxic we are making it. As a result, we fear hearing the news that our bodies have finally paid the price for our mindless way of living.

Consider this unorthodox health exam I've devised, which I have based on my own contrary thinking about what it means to live a healthy life. It may give you a new perspective on your health and a renewed sense of determination to pursue a savored existence:

1. *Are you experiencing chest pleasures?* Do you feel warmth and openness in your chest when you witness acts of great kindness and caring?

2. *Have you lost your senses?* Can you get so involved in something you enjoy that you lose all sense of time, space, and self?

3. *Do you ignore most risk factors?* Are you living your life in accordance with your own principles, values, and mindful consideration of data rather than in compliance with someone else's warnings about what might kill you?

4. *Are you experiencing repeated bouts of benefit-finding?* Even at your sickest moments, are you able to find meaning in illness that might enhance your own life and the lives of your family members?

5. *Have you lost your sense of self?* Do you view your health as related to how you interact with your family, others, and the world and not just how you personally feel and look?

6. *Have you a noticed bright discoloration of your dark days?* Do you fully appreciate your days even when you are ill and relish those days when you feel just "pretty good?"

7. *Are you experiencing frequent bouts of dizziness brought on by contradictory health warnings?* Are you free of "health guilt" and concern that you have directly caused the symptoms you may experience by not thinking the right way?

8. *Have you noticed persistent signs of deep connection?* Do you see health not just as existing within one person but between all persons?

I know of few medical conditions that would cause anyone to score low on this test. Even those of us who are seriously ill can still be healthy according to my test.

FIVE PROPOSITIONS ABOUT HEALTH AND HEALING

To help you relieve yourself of some of the guilt engendered by modern medicine and the pressure to self-heal, here are a few propositions related to health. Remember, many self-help books that deal with physical health issues don't pay much attention to love, familying, or working. They usually take on one particular health issue, but health and illness take place within systems. I hope you will think back on the propositions you have read so far as you think about what it means to be healthy.

Health Proposition Number One: Illness is essential to your health. We can cure many diseases, but we seldom ask why disease exists. If evolution can produce the remarkable immune and healing systems within our bodies, why hasn't it done away with disease? What is illness for? The researchers Randolph Nesse and George Williams introduced the new field of Darwinian medicine to address just these questions.[15] Their research suggests that we become ill so that we can be healthy. So long as we learn to overcome our illnesses, survival of the illest might be an evolutionary principle.

When you are feverish or tired, your immune system is defending you against millions of tiny invaders; feeling unwell is a sign that you need to rest. Nausea shows that the body needs to purge itself of something that might damage it. Sickness is a necessary human response to illness—it is not an enemy against which we must always do battle.

Feeling terrible reminded me more than anything else that I was still alive; and one of the surprising signs that my health was improving was that I appeared to be getting sicker. I had been so heavily medicated during the worst of my illness that I often felt numb. All sorts of discomforts returned as the medications were reduced, and as bothersome as they were, I grew to appreciate and endure them as signs that I was becoming healthy enough to feel sick again.

Health Proposition Number Two: Indulgence is good.   The message behind many health warnings is that pleasure is bad and early death is avoided by denying what we crave. Pleasure would not have survived evolution if was not essential to our health. If something tastes, feels, or smells good to you, indulge yourself. The trick isn't denial, it's pacing. Fill your life with as many guilty pleasures as possible and relish a smug deviant guilt while doing it. Feel some savoring shame as you watch health fanatics being horrified but jealous by your escape from health terrorism.

Indulgence is good for our health in the long run if we remember the pleasure prescription: Savor slowly, pace yourself, and seek variety. Research shows that the "moderation in all things" we're supposed to practice is achieved by fully and slowly experiencing each indulgence, not by suppressing our natural savoring responses.[16] If you love chocolate, engage in a little mindful munching. Take a small nibble, then fully and lingeringly taste it until the taste has gone. Now comes the hard part. Wait a "moderation minute." Don't take another bite for sixty seconds. This might seem like forever, but you may not crave another bite. If you do want another one, savor it, but pace yourself again before taking more. Finally, seek out different shapes and varieties of chocolate. Try as many guilty pleasures as possible, enjoy them all slowly, and spread them out. This approach reduces the habituation to pleasure that leads us to the overindulgence and unconscious automatic face filling that *is* a risk to health.

Based on my reading of the research, my own health program is still the SWELMM approach: Savor Well, Eat Less, Move More. I'm not suggesting that smoking, drinking to excess, not exercising, or eating a lot of fatty junk food isn't bad for us. I am suggesting that health is much simpler than we imagine; we just have to stop doing the obviously stupid things and start doing smarter things such as eating, drinking, and exercising with the enlightened savoring that comes from a more mindful life. We are nowhere near as vulnerable as the health terrorists say we are. Comedian Johnny Carson illustrated the perspective of balancing pleasure with prudence when he joked, "I once knew a man who gave up smoking, drinking, and sex. He was healthy right up to the day he killed himself."

Health Proposition Number Three: There is no such thing as an illness-causing emotion.   During my illness, I experienced a wide range of emotions. Some of my moods no doubt made my wife contemplate euthanasia as an option for putting an end to my whining and grousing, but none of my so-called negative emotions did me in. I am convinced that when it comes to our emotional health, there are no sickness-inducing emotions, only "stuck" emotions. Sometimes when I was gravely ill, I would get stuck for a long time in a really down mood, but I learned to wait those times out and even learned during and from them. I learned to stop trying to impose my own time limit on the law of emotional dynamics—what goes down will eventually go up. I have discovered the reason we die. It's not because of our emotions, attitudes, or thinking styles. It's because we're mortal.

No emotional state lasts, and that includes happiness. No matter how down or up I feel, that emotion is by its very nature ephemeral. I'm reminded of something Adam Smith wrote in 1759, in *The Theory of Moral Sentiments*: "The mind of every man, in a longer or shorter time, returns to its natural and usual state of tranquility. In prosperity, after a certain time, it falls back to that state; in adversity, after a certain time, it rises up to it." The only "negative" emotion is a "stuck" emotion. The lower an emotion, the higher will be the high emotion. The higher an emotion, the lower will be the inevitable low emotion that follows. Although it's difficult always to remember, I learned during my illness that it was natural that the lower I felt, the higher I would eventually feel later.

Today, I try to remember to savor my high moments while they last because I know that an equally intense low emotion must inevitably follow. It's impossible—and exhaustingly unhealthy—to be up all the time. It may not be "the" good life, but to have our own good one, we have to learn to savor as much of life, good and bad, as we can. Self-help's happiness ethic wreaks havoc on our emotional lives because it pushes us to achieve an emotional state that will never last and—even if we could attain such a long high—the law of emotional dynamics guarantees a huge and long emotional crash.

Health Proposition Number Four: A positive attitude is not necessary for healing.   For her studies of optimism, Suzanne C. Segerstrom won the largest cash prize in psychology, the 2002 Templeton Positive Psychology Prize. Her studies showed that the constant effort to maintain a positive and upbeat attitude is not necessarily the best way to engage in healing and it may even waste precious healing energy; the studies also showed that good old-fashioned kvetching can promote the healing process and that there can be adaptive positive power in negative thinking.

Segerstrom's work showed that the view of life that relentlessly accentuates the positive and eliminates the negative is not the best way to heal. Sometimes, particularly anxious negative thinking in the form of what one psychologist called "defensive pessimism" helps them as much as "strategic optimism."[17] Going over negative consequences can be as instructively healing as visualizing wonderful ones.

If there is a healing optimism, it's the kind that mindfully looks at all sides. It also focuses on the dark side, the negative information and events that happen in all our lives and from which we can learn. It takes that information and, often with the help of others, construes it in such a way that we can select and mix and match from our three healing strengths of fighting, quitting, and growing. It is this kind of thinking—a person's cool-and-know optimism, not the hot-and-go relentless and often forced positive attitude approach—that leads to a strengthened immune system, more rapid recovery from surgery, and a longer and healthier life.[18]

Health Proposition Number Five: Giving up is essential to healing. The process of healing is enhanced when we have a sense of control over our situation, but, as you have read, control is not always gained by unrelenting effort toward a goal. Sometimes we can assume control of our challenge by abandoning our pursuit of it. Giving up is not the same as assuming a helpless orientation to our adversity.[19] It is important to make a clear distinction between "not trying anymore" and totally relinquishing our commitment to our original healing goal. If we simply reduce our effort while remaining single-mindedly committed to our original objective, we can end up feeling helplessly trapped in struggle mode, unable to turn away from the goal, a stressful state not at all conducive to healing.[20]

Our grandest goals can become the greatest obstacles to savoring the grandeur of daily living. One of my own original goals was not only to survive cancer but also never to be in pain again. I know now how foolishly selfish that goal was. I know that pain is as essential to a full life as is pleasure. Now I see pain—every headache and every sore muscle—as a reminder that I'm alive. Like the wonderful pleasures of my life, I have learned that pain is like life itself. It's by its very nature ephemeral.

∽

I have come to think of being healthy as the same as being mindful: being fully mentally engaged in all that life offers. I tried to think of my illness as part of a system instead of just a predicament I was experiencing alone. I did a lot of mindful cool and knowing thinking about ways to heal, and my wife and I sought second, third, fourth, and tenth opinions from experts, their published research, and, most of all, from my loving family and friends. I did a lot of positive and negative thinking and found solace and new lessons by sometimes being a world-class kvetcher. I came to view health as retaining control of my consciousness and being mindful even when pain was so demanding of my attention. I saw it as retaining a feeling of being connected even when illness tore my body apart and I learned that there is no one way to think or feel, no one set of things to do, in order to have health. Being healthy has more to do with mindful being that effortful doing.

Overcoming the Burden of Youth

I'm growing old! I'm falling apart! And it's very interesting!

WILLIAM SAROYAN

PROPOSITIONS ABOUT AGING

1. More young people die than older people.
2. Successful aging is not staying young.
3. Older people are less depressed than younger people.
4. Older people are more sexually content than younger people.
5. Old age and bad health are not related.

THE GIFT OF A THIRD LIFETIME

What do you consider the most important breakthroughs of the twentieth century? Putting a man on the moon, the advent of computers, air travel? As important as these achievements are, they pale in comparison to the one accomplishment that makes all the others worthwhile: the addition of thirty years to the life spans of most Americans. In effect, we have been given a third lifetime to add on to youth and middle age.

For the first time in history, the majority of those born in the Western world will survive into old age.[1] Children born today have a reasonable chance of living to be a hundred years old. A child born in 1900 could hope for only half as much. There is no doubt that life spans are lengthening. But living a long life is one thing. Living a satisfying long life, one that encompasses years of mindful living, is another.

Pointing out the danger of viewing aging as a battle to stay young, the gerontologist Walter Bortz warned that we can end up living too short and dying too long.[2] He nicely captured self-potentialism's ideal of "healthy aging" as not really aging at all. Knowing how to savor the magnificent gift of thirty more years of life and flourish through them requires a profound shift in the way we think about the meanings and manifestations of growing old. We need to reject the notion of an "ageless body and a timeless mind."

Whether we end up struggling to survive or learning to thrive through our gift years is largely a matter of not only accepting but appreciating the changes that time writes on our bodies and minds. Thriving entails losing the fear, for example, that our memories are dimming; we should consider instead whether some memory loss might not be a good thing. Perhaps the gradual erosion of short-term recall allows us to attend more fully to our present living. Thriving in old age means giving up the struggle to maintain a taut, young body; it means considering the notion that the aches and pains we accumulate along with our birthdays might be nature's own way of saying sit down, shut up, and savor life.

Most of the self-help gurus of "healthy aging" are relatively young. Their fear of what comes naturally with advancing years is evident in their recommendations about how to live longer yet avoid looking or feeling older. To have a good long life, it is wiser to consider the lessons of the *real* experts on joyful aging, the savoring seniors who have learned how to relish the third lifetime in their own ways.

If we are to become more mindful about aging, we must heed the advice of Socrates: "I enjoy talking with very old people. They have gone before us on a road by which we, too, may have to travel, and I think we do well to learn from them what it is like." One wise ninety-year-old confessed that she'd taken all her self-help books on how not to look old, how to be fit and stay young, and how to be a sexy senior and tied them together into two packs: "I carry them around in each arm a few times a day," she said. "It's great exercise and better for me than trying to do what they tell me to do." Another thriving senior, a man of eighty-six, told me, "It's strange to me that all the young people are buying books on how to learn to slow down, calm down, meditate, and take time to enjoy life. Having an old mind and body makes you do that automatically. You have to move and think slow. If you ask me, that mind/body new age stuff should explain how to follow the wisdom of your body. Young people should learn from us and watch how we live. We're doing what they say they want to do."

Writing in 1874, when people were old at age forty, author Henri Amiel said, "To know how to grow old is the master-work of wisdom, and one of the most difficult chapters in the great art of living." Our youth-obsessed society has made that chapter of life unnecessarily difficult.

I recently saw a full-page advertisement for Botox, a poisonous chemical injected into the face to reduce temporarily the appearance of wrinkles. The ad showed a man and woman who appeared to be in their late twenties. The caption said, "We promised to grow old together, not look old together." God forbid we should look our age!

Clinging to self-helpism's perpetual pubescence, we prefer to be closet seniors who know we are old but don't want to "come out" for fear of suffering the discrimination associated with age. We swell with pride when we are told we look younger than we are; but we are hurt when someone says, "You're really showing your age." And indeed, the prejudice against age is real—but the only way to beat it is to buck it.

As with any other type of discrimination, ageism will not vanish so long as people kowtow to it.

The self-help movement did not invent the obsession with youth, but it embraces and perpetuates it. Self-helpism equates youth with self-actualization and implies that the struggle to stay young is the only way to lead the good life. To self-potentialists, admitting that you "feel old" is tantamount to an admission of failure to eat properly, work out enough, or nurture a "young attitude." As one of my senior patients pointed out, "I'm seventy-six and I look it and feel it. I don't want to look and feel young. I've been there and done that. Now I'm trying out another time of life, and even if young people don't know it yet, it's at least as wonderful as feeling young."

Even though the alternative to aging is dying, few us are willing to accept nature's toll for traveling the longer life road. Take, for example, the term "old fogy." "Fogy" refers to someone who is rigid in his or her ways, highly opinionated, and not up to speed on the most current information. By this definition, my experience is that there are at least as many "young fogies" as old ones, but the prejudice against age is pervasive.

Modern Western psychology forgets that it is only the most recent version of the attempt to understand the human mind; it often suffers from a cultural myopia in its neglect of how ancient cultures treasured age. The West's glorification of youth, its admiration for youthful looks and behavior, and its discrimination against older people in the workplace differs from Eastern and my own Hawaiian culture's admiration of elders and the desire to learn from and be guided by them.

Thanks to ageism, much less is known about the last thirty years of life than the first five. This is because most researchers are either relatively young or are not facing the reality of their own aging. Gerontologists study the old as separate "subjects" who are distant from them and going through a process that they hope to prevent if possible, delay if they can, and treat with hundreds of medications.

The arm's-length approach to aging was illustrated in my conversation with a well-known thirty-six-year-old gerontologist. When I asked him why he was interested in researching aging, he answered, "Because someday I'm going to be aging, too." He was taken aback when I asked, "And on what day of your life did you *stop* getting older?"

Like most physicians, medical researchers try to figure out how to avoid suffering rather than promote savoring. Either by temperament or training, they are consumed with looking for problems rather than benefits. They focus on vulnerabilities associated with the aging process rather than new strengths that can emerge because of it. Their blindness to the opportunities offered by age causes them to miss the calmness and the salutary effects that can be of benefit to young and old alike. Their inattentiveness causes them to overlook the fact that the old can relish memories not available to the young, and indeed, contemplate where they have been instead of where they are going.

WHAT'S WRONG WITH LOOKING YOUR AGE?

Self-helpism suffers from fears that research shows that most old people don't experience: concerns about death, loneliness, and depression. The longest study of aging ever conducted, the Study of Adult Development at Harvard University, showed that most old people report having no desire to be young again, are less afraid of death than young people, have just the right number of friends and plenty of good memories of past associations, and often feel better about their lives than their younger counterparts. And yet the supreme compliment for someone who has tapped into the glories of the gift years is "My, you don't at all look your age!"

The fact remains, however, that no matter how much hair dye, wrinkle cream, vitamins, and herbs we use, most people do look their age. It would be unthinkable to say, "Hi. You're looking nice and old today." By accepting the taboos against this kind of truth telling, and the rule that "age equals ugly," we are complicit in looks-based discrimination.

When I was ill, I would have given anything to look old. I told one of my doctors that I had found the ultimate antiaging treatment—undergoing intense chemotherapy. When I looked in the mirror, my steroid-altered baby face and chemotherapy-induced baldness suddenly made me look much younger than my forty-seven years. I joked that I had received a complete medical makeover, including a chemotherapy face-lift, cancer hair cut, and radiation tummy tuck. When I look at pictures from that time, I am struck by the paradox that the cancer growing uncontrollably within me was crowding out the natural aging processes that so many healthy people avoid so aggressively.

I was amused by some of the older male doctors who obviously dyed their hair. With their fifty-year-old faces and eighteen-year-old hair they looked more like puppets than people. When I saw female staff and visitors who had undergone face-lifts and other age-defying plastic surgeries, I thought they looked neither young nor old. They just looked strange and stretched.

Why aren't they showing off their age instead of trying to hide it? I wondered. *If I live long enough to get wrinkles, I'm going to show them off. Getting older is an accomplishment and a blessing, not a failure and a curse.*

George Burns, the famous comedian, served as one of the best examples of a person who had an aging body and loved every minute of being in it. He aged mindfully and in his own way, free of the pressures of self-helpism. When Burns was ninety-five, a researcher asked him what his doctor said about his smoking and drinking. With his inimitable timing and humor, he answered, "My doctor is dead."

AGING IS A LAUGHING MATTER

As George Burns has demonstrated, a good sense of humor is a fundamental characteristic of age. That's because old people have lived long enough to realize just how ridiculous life can be and how silly our self-importance, illusion of personal control, and efforts to look and feel young forever really are. One of my oldest patients was a ninety-nine-year-old retired physician. She had just come from her physical exam with a young medical student and she told me, "You had better go and comfort that young man. He seemed awfully upset." When I asked what had happened, she said she had asked the medical student why he didn't ask her about her sex life. He had looked embarrassed, so to relax him, she had told him a joke. She asked him, "What's the difference between a tire and 365 condoms?" When he said he didn't know, she told him, "When you think of a tire, you think of a *Goodyear*. When you think of 365 condoms, you think of a *great* year." At that point, the doctor had dropped his stethoscope and left the exam room.

I asked my secretary to bring me the patient's medical chart. The young physician had written, "Patient expresses inappropriate thoughts regarding sexuality." When I read that passage to her, she laughed and said, "Poor man. He's clearly not ready to be old or to help anyone who is."

GERONTOLOGY OR PATHOLOGY?

Gerontology is really "geronto-pathology." As a medical field, it considers the signs of aging to be symptoms that we are suffering from "old-timer's" disease. The new self-potentialism buzz phrase is "successful aging," and dozens of new self-help books are coming out to appeal to aging baby boomers. These books present various ways of doing everything and almost anything possible not to age. A serious flaw of self-helpism is that it focuses on that perpetual inner child while demanding that we never show our outer elder.

Like any good self-help program, medicine for aging patients is almost exclusively oriented toward repair and prevention. The implication is that aging is a disease that can be treated. Middle-age standards of health are being applied to later-age patients, and the natural changes that accompany aging are seen as signs that we have failed in the quest for eternal youth.

Most older people will suffer some degree of arthritis. By declaring arthritis a disease, we are labeling the vast majority of seniors as sick. Despite the array of drugs designed to treat arthritis, the condition is a natural consequence of old bones and joints. All old living beings grow stiff. The serious negative side effects of the medications given to help arthritis can in themselves make old age less enjoyable. Most of us will ache, sag, and hurt as we grow older. As one of my patients said, "Why does my doctor want to keep me in middle age? That just leaves me in the middle. I want to enjoy old age now and I don't want to be drugged up so much that I can't pay attention to my life before I don't have it anymore. Besides, all my friends are old. . . . I don't want to stick out."

Most of the medicines piled high on the tables of the elderly were never tested on the older people taking them. As in most research protocols, the drugs were tested mostly on young white men, a few white women, and a lot of white rats, but not many people with white hair. Modern medicine trusts almost exclusively in what it calls randomized controlled trials, but people older than seventy-five are rarely found in these trials. In effect, older people have become guinea pigs involuntarily involved in a massive field experiment: the testing of drugs that may or may not be of help to those who become old in the future.

Some facts of aging will not change no matter how much medicine we take or how much we keep a positive attitude and a youthful outlook: No amount of trying to think and behave as we did when we were much younger changes the fact that we will grow old. I want to live a good old life, not strive for a self-potentialism illusion of a perpetually younger one.

After surviving my own brush with death, I have absolutely no desire to "think young" now. I cherish the opportunity to be my age, or even a

little older if I can. For people who have not yet had the painful benefit of facing their own mortality, I suggest you take a moment to sit
down and ask yourself this question: "If God gave me the choice between dying young or suddenly looking and feeling old but living a long
and active life, which would I choose?" For most people, the choice is
for a long old life. For many older people I interviewed, being young
was nice, but not always all that nice. As one of my older patients
pointed out, "Being young is foreplay for really living."

Although we might not enjoy facing the following facts of old age, no
magical elixir, positive thinking, or amount of personal power will significantly change the aging events. Take a hard look at reality:

- More than half of us will have the aches and pains of various
  degrees and kinds of arthritis.
- Digesting food will become more difficult.
- Our hearing will diminish.
- Our short-term memory will diminish.
- Our skin will sag and our wrinkles will deepen.
- We will nap more.
- Age spots will form on our faces and other areas of our bodies.
  (These are actually "stress spots" from the reduced metabolism
  of stress hormones and long exposure to them.)
- The genders will merge in appearance, the differences between
  old men and old women being less obvious.
- As the Earth beckons us back to it, our bodies will react to
  gravity's insistent pull by bending us over.
- We will move more slowly and have more trouble getting up.

As I think about these inevitable changes, it's as if nature were trying to tell me something not only about how to age gracefully but also
about how to live joyfully. These harsh facts serve as invitations to leading the good life right now no matter how old we are.

- If you hurt, don't take a medicine. Take a nap.
- Stop eating so much rich and spicy food.
- Say less and listen more.
- Relish your long-term memories, value creating them, and worry less about short-term memory.
- Worry less about how you look.
- Don't waste too much time sleeping.
- See your age spots as badges representing a fully engaged life well lived.
- Realize how similar you are to everyone else, man or woman.
- Sit down. Stay put. You can't get there from "not here."
- Slow down. You've been going too fast anyway.

Nature might be trying to apply the brakes to all our mindless and hectic lives by making it more and more difficult to lead such a life. The signs of aging could be templates of how best to live from day to day. Nature is trying to awaken our "codger consciousness" by persuading us to sit down long enough to pay attention to the wisdom that comes from an older mind. When young people become impatient with the slow-moving old people in front of them in line, they should take a mindful moment and ask themselves whether they aren't being presented with a message about how to lead their own lives. Nature is saying that it is time to be much more mindful of life well lived before it is too late.

FEELING OUR AGE AND SAVORING IT

Although self-helpism constantly insists that "age is a state of mind," it isn't. Aging is a natural process. The constant reminder to "think young!" implies that "old thinking" is not as valuable as "young think-ing." I'm not sure that I'm all that pleased with some of my young thinking and what it led to. At sixty-two, I want to *think* that age. I want a mature mind that matches up with its body.

The author Cora Harvey Armstrong wrote, "Inside every old person is a younger person wondering 'What the hell happened?'" If we aren't ready for what the aging process does to us and cling desperately to trying to look young, growing old can happen overnight. Despite doing all the right things and following all the right steps, one day we will look in the mirror and ask, "When did I get old?" The answer is that we are always getting old, and we're often too hurried to savor the process or too selfishly foolish to appreciate the opportunity to do so.

Those of us who are older have the opportunity to be bichronological, meaning that we can sometimes engage a younger mind and at other times think with a senior mind. Unlike the young, we know what it is like to be old as well as young. But I'm not sure that it's a compliment to tell an eighty-year-old person that she or he "still thinks like a forty-year-old."

SAME PERSON, DIFFERENT BODY

Most of the older people I've interviewed say that they feel no different from when they were younger. Their core identity had not changed. Some elders say they can think both "old" and "young" and that this allows them to think more creatively and with less concern for conformity. Because there is less of it left, they feel more excited about the life to which they are grateful to awaken every day. Now that I'm older, I never get up when I wake up. I always take several minutes to lie there and relish the gift of being alive.

There is nothing sick or wrong with a senior consciousness and an old body. No one points to a young child and says, "Poor child. Look how terribly soft and undefined his skin is." No one says about a successful young executive, "How terrible that such a young woman thinks so quickly and responds so fast."

Our consciousness develops, but it doesn't age in the same way as our bodies. Within a narrow range, nature establishes the timetable for the aging of the body. Exercise, diet, and meditate as we will, there is really not much we can do to reset that clock. Deepak Chopra is wrong when he says we have ageless bodies, but he's right when he says we have timeless minds.

In a sense, time is the ultimate criterion of health. I don't mean stopping or turning back time by using a "mind over matter" approach so that we can live in an unblemished state of perpetual youth. I'm referring to the idea, not easily accepted in Western cultures, that there are two kinds of time. One is often called "profane" or "monochromic," which is linear clock time. It's the "normal" view of time, the one we take when we see sand running through the hourglass, or minutes ticking away. It's the time expressed in Shakespeare's *Richard II*: "I wasted time, and now doth time waste me."

The other time, the time we ourselves determine, is "sacred" or "polychronic" time: It's the time we determine by what we elect to put into our consciousness. We have the capacity to set the tempo of our lives through how we choose to attend to it, and the potential of joy in our aging rests in our willingness to take charge of our own consciousness and not allow it to be driven by events. Moreover, if we elect to remain mentally flexible and embrace, rather than fear, the aging process, we will have the option of employing a bichronological consciousness, one that affords us two perspectives on life—one derived from thinking like a young person, the other derived from the wisdom accrued with age.

My cancer had prematurely aged my body, but I was still essentially the same person I was before cancer did its damage. As cancer accelerated my aging process at frightening speed, I could still see that I could become much wiser as an old person than I was when I was young. I could be free of the demands of time because I could control it with how I thought about the world around me. I'm much more interested now in thinking slowly and for longer and in trying to be wiser. I know that reflection, character, judgment, and connective thinking are as important as potentialism's quick individual thinking, high self-esteem, personal power, and the confident declarative ideas about what *should* constitute the good life.

I don't think the wisdom of aging comes from knowing more but from finally admitting what we don't know and never will. I've learned that I don't need to give in to the self-help nagging of trying to have it all. Looking back at my years, I realize that I always did. It is through this wise surrender of certainty that we can learn to stop using just one of our three human strengths, perseverance, and look to the other two—growth and the ability to give in and give up. We can grow through our aging when we stop fighting against its signs and give in to them. We can use our other two strengths by continuing to grow through our later years in our own ways and by surrendering the illusion that we have anywhere near the control over destiny as the personal-power concept asserts.

THE CIRCLE OF OLD LIFE

Many of us spend the first twenty years of our lives surviving, the next twenty striving, the next twenty arriving, and our gift of an extra thirty more years back in surviving mode. As I have described in the chapters about loving, familying, working, thriving, and healing, leading our own good life depends on avoiding the mindless acceptance of a set of "facts" about an older life. You read in Chapter 3 that research by Fred Bryant and Joseph Veroff has established the new field of study called "savoring." They define the savoring response as full conscious attention to life as it is and avoiding constant planning for a future that arrived yesterday. Their findings show that basking in what we have already achieved, giving thanks for the opportunity to achieve it, luxuriating by indulging the senses, and particularly *marveling* at the wonder of the moment are the key components of savoring. Being older affords us the history and experience to do these things.

One of self-helpism's belief biases that interferes with savoring our seniority is that life goes by in stages, step-by-step. Popular psychology classifies humans into categories according to age. It sees us as toddlers, infants, children, adolescents, young adults, middle-aged, and then as the dreaded old-aged. It establishes an illusionary and savoring-limiting consciousness boundary between being young and growing old, but few of us can remember crossing the barrier.

Most of us don't experience life in stages. Instead, we are constantly cycling around within the experience of living. As my wife and I celebrated our fortieth wedding anniversary, we came to see life more as a circle than as a staircase. The saying "The more things change, the more they stay the same" applies to our experience of life. We go through the best of times, then the worst of times, then again the best of times. If there are "passages" in life, we keep walking around and around in them instead of up and through them. We celebrate and grieve again and again.

It's only when a much younger person lets me know how old I look that I remember how old my body has become. I usually feel that I am consciously interacting with the world at various times and in various situations in a childish, adolescent, middle-aged, or old-aged way. I'm not interested in being any age for very long. I'm busy doing something I feared I never would. I'm getting older and older by the moment and loving every minute of it.

I've been twice blessed. I have come back from the brink of death and also been allowed the chance to savor the thirty-year gift I feared I would never have. As I've thought about aging since my illness, I have come to savor and wonder in it. I know that, like almost everyone else, no matter how many self-help programs we try, I will suffer from at least some degree of hardening of the arteries. My joints will grow stiff, but my thinking doesn't have to become rigid. I can suffer from the hardening of the arteries that comes with getting old without experiencing hardening of my attitudes about aging.

It isn't aging that threatens the quality of life; it's the failure to be mindfully engaged in all that life offers us no matter how old we are. I don't think there is any such thing as a mid-life or late-life crisis, only a whole-life crisis to which we finally awaken, and that crisis is usually our failure to pay attention to sharing a savored life.

GRAYING OR GLOWING?

Chemotherapy caused me to lose all my hair. Even most of my body hair disappeared. When the hair grew back on my head, I thought it had turned gray. I was wrong. As it turns out, I was beginning to glow old.

Our hair does not turn gray; it literally begins to glow. As we age, our individual hairs lose the inner protein matrix that gives them color. In effect, they become hollow. This allows a tiny shaft of light to enter each hair, causing a silver halo around our heads. Whether we are radiating with wisdom or showing our light-headedness about our aging depends on whether we are willing to learn the real facts of aging and put our minds to what we are experiencing. As for myself, I have found great relief in giving up trying to stay young. I now understand the psychologist William James's statement: "How pleasant is the day when we give up our striving to be young and slender. Thank God, we say, those illusions are gone. Everything added to the self is a burden as well as a pride."

One of my patients was Harold, a ninety-year-old retired physicist who had worked for the federal government. He had come to see me in my role as a neuropsychologist at Sinai Hospital of Detroit. His physician told me that he thought his old patient was "failing mentally." Harold was a grouchy man with very little patience. His wife said, "He's not an old grump, he's just a grump. He always has been. That's not because he's old. It's because he's him." When I told him that I thought it was a waste of his time for me to conduct further tests on him, Harold agreed. He said, "Why do people say you are failing when you are getting old? Nobody says newborn babies are failing because they cry and pee all over themselves. That's just how they are. Well, I'm ninety and I'm how I am. Most of me isn't old anyway. I'm a physicist and I know we're all made up of 98 percent water and I've never heard of old water. I'm made up of atoms, and atoms are 99 percent space. There's no such thing as old space. It's my doctor who is failing—failing to accept the changes of aging. That's his problem, not mine."

As the couple left my office, the wife softly punched her husband's arm. She was a retired nurse who had spent years working on a geron-tology unit at the local hospital. With mock anger and loud enough so that my secretary and I could hear, she said, "See. I told you my diag-nosis was right. You were a young pain in the ass, a middle-aged pain in the ass, and now you're an old pain in the ass." As the door closed, we could hear their laughter as they walked down the hall.

FIVE PROPOSITIONS ABOUT AGING

When I lecture about aging, I ask my audience to think about how old they are emotionally. They often chuckle at that question, but it's as important as how many years we have lived. Have your emotions kept up with your years? Have you gone beyond childish defensiveness? Are you becoming calmer, less reactive, more patient, and are you a lit-tle wiser, or at least try to be? Have you overcome the burden of im-pulsive youthful self-absorption? How you answer these questions is as important to healthy aging as being free of disease and bodily aches and pains.

Aging Proposition Number One: More young people die than older people.   As you get older, death changes from something that might happen to something that will happen. My ninety-three-year-old Hawaiian friend is a *kupuna*, a revered elder. He spoke of his acceptance of endings when he said, "I knew I had gone from younger to older when I started noticing sunsets more than sunrises. I don't see anything less beautiful about them, but I watch the horizon more now for the sun setting than for it rising. I think it's just as nice a way of looking at the world as looking only for sunrises, but I am aware that it is a sunset. That doesn't make me feel sad. It just makes me feel."

It's true that genetics play an important role in determining our life spans. (I joke with my students that if their parents did not have children, they won't, either.) Having two parents who lived into their eighties adds on average about three years to our life expectancy, but the quality of the other twenty-seven of our bonus thirty years are very much up to us.

Only 1 percent of deaths are due purely to old age.[3] Just read the daily paper and you will see that many more young people die than much older people. George Burns claimed that he looked forward to being one hundred years old because he didn't know many people who had died at that age. Associating death purely with aging is a needless waste of life-savoring time. Trying to outexercise or undereat death can block our chances of enjoying the years we have.

The healthiest and happiest older people I've talked with were much less concerned with issues of death than the younger people with whom I spoke. Aging, then, isn't moving closer to dying; it's an opportunity to grow much closer to living.

Aging Proposition Number Two: Successful aging is not staying young.   Research shows that the majority of Americans under the age of fifty think that the best times for everything important in life are before age fifty.[4] They've been indoctrinated by potentialism's gerontophobia. They fail to see that the rewards of lasting intimate relationships, of watching children grow and flourish, of feeling secure and successful in our work, all require a history, not just goals.

We experience some hearing loss as we age because nature knows that there is too much noise in the world and it's time we enjoyed a little peace and quiet. Perhaps a little slipping of attention is provided for us by nature because so much of the information clutter of the world isn't worth our full attention—and isn't very useful in the first place.

The insistence on perpetual youth is perverse to me. It's like working for fifty years only to deny yourself a retirement party, or slogging through a long winter only to fly north when spring comes. We do our best to grow and learn throughout childhood and young adulthood so that we can relish the fruits of our labor during our gift years. Successful aging means bidding a cheerful farewell to youth, not clinging to it desperately.

Aging Proposition Number Three: Older people are less depressed than younger people.   Despite the immense number of antidepressants dispensed to old people, clinically diagnosable depression is much less prevalent in older people than in young adults.[5] Much of the sadness older people experience is the perfectly natural response to the world's rejection of them.

Much of the depression for which seniors are medicated is not the kind of depression for which those drugs were intended. It is a depression associated with being denied the opportunity to be who and how they are and the freedom to engage in life their own way. Although an active retirement may be the good life for some seniors, there is nothing wrong with a passive, reflective good old life, either. If our own or others' ideas of what retirement should be are imposed upon us, depression is the likely reaction.

It's important to point out that there isn't anything wrong with being depressed. Life and its transitions can be sad. Crying, moping, and feeling sorry for ourselves when we're any age is not being "dysfunctional." It's being human. Despite the happiology of self-help, sometimes it is necessary, healthy, and healing to submit to a blue mood. So long as we are not stuck in a chronically depressed state, feeling blue and reflecting life's tribulations can lead to creative thinking. Sometimes people aren't depressed because they *fail* to face reality but because they do.

That seniors tend to have more "cool and slow" rather than "hot and go" emotions of younger people can be frustrating to the hurried young people running around them, and younger physicians often mistake this for clinical depression; "cool and slow" is, however, a natural feature of growing older.

The Harvard study on aging discovered that depression in seniors is rare and often misdiagnosed. Research on aging and depression summarized by the psychologist William A. Sadler showed that conditions that limit time tend to deepen the complexity of our thinking and emotions, but deep thinking is not sad thinking. The "hot and go" style of thinking characteristic of the young sees reflective and contemplative thought as a sign of depression, and mistakes depth and complexity for sluggish and senile. The time that old people take to pay attention is often mistaken for confusion by younger people unaware of the point made by the psychologist Tom Peters: "If you're not confused, you're not paying attention."

Research also shows that older people show a richer and deeper range of emotions than young people. Their goals tend to change from seeking mental uproar to slowly appreciating meaning, historical perspective, and stability. That's not depression. It's wisdom.

Deep emotional closeness with family members and friends also increases with age. Old people may have fewer casual acquaintances, but they generally have closer friends than younger people. The narrowing of their friendship circle is less a matter of friends dying off than putting off those who they think are only wasting their time. Older people engage in a kind of "people pruning" through which they parcel out their socialization time where, when, and with whom they feel it matters most.

Older people are not just concerned with seeking happiness. They are able to mix joy and sadness into one cherished feeling in the present moment. When I was forced by my cancer to think older, I was surprised how little most of us know about the present moment. Young relatives of my older patients often point out that a grandmother or grandfather "drifts off," but they are often tuning in to the present moment so fully that it can frustrate those who are in a hurry to get to the next.

Those who interact regularly with old people tell me that their senior relatives often cry "for no reason." They are wrong. My interviews, and research by the psychologist Rocio Fernandez-Bellesterosa, indicate that old people cry for reasons not easily understood by the young. Their tears flow from a blend of reflective loving memories and the suddenly intense savoring of a moment in time. Their memories result in an emotional poignancy related to their awareness not only of the magnificence of life but of its brevity and fragility.

Aging Proposition Number Four: Older people are more sexually content than younger people.   From what I've heard coming out of the mouths of young men I know, there would be at least as many "dirty young men" as old, but they are more easily forgiven for their impetuous and lustful ways than their elders, who are seen as lecherous old geezers. Young couples who publicly demonstrate their love are thought of as romantic. Old couples displaying affection are seen as "cute," "remarkable for their age," or, as one of my young medical students put it, "kind of weird."

Perhaps one of the most pervasive misconceptions about older life is that if old people are to be active sexual beings, they need help. The assumption is that interest and sexual performance decreases as we get older. Again, research does not support this "fact" of old life. Older people report maintaining their sexual interest far into their later years and that they have much more time to think about and enjoy sex than they did when they were young.

One of my patients, Marge, was an eighty-six-year-old woman. She described her sex life this way: "My hubby and I don't have sex like young people. Hell, we wouldn't want to. I think young people should try to have sex like us old people. They should take it slower, easier, and think less about their genitals and more about their relationships. I think they should take a lot more time and be much more careful about it. You have to go a little slower when you're older, and I think it makes it better. They should try a little senior sex sometime."

There is no doubt that having good sex is good for our health. Regular sexual activity reduces our chances of dying young. A ten-year British study of 3,500 men and women showed that those older people who reported having regular sex were in better general health than those who did not. The study showed that they also gained the societal bonus of having others say that they looked "seven to ten years younger than their actual age," but as one of my patients said, "I don't have sex to look young. I do it because it feels good." The French film actress Jeanne Moreau suggested that age does not protect us from love, but love protects us from age. Having sex may not really protect us from aging, but it can make it much more enjoyable.

Aging Proposition Number Five: Old age and bad health are not related.   Most adults older than age sixty-five are remarkably healthy.[6] Contrary to what you might see in television commercials advertising drugs for seniors, most old people are not sick people. More than 90 percent of the very old do not live in nursing homes, and 73 percent of adults ages seventy-eight to eighty-four report having no disabling conditions. Almost half of those older than eighty-five do not have physical or mental problems that limit their daily living.[7] Contrary to what you might have heard about the exploding elderly population, we are not on the brink of geriatric Armageddon.

Old people are not about to burden the world by becoming millions of greedy geezers so medically needy that they drain the medical and financial resources of the young. If seniors consume billions of dollars worth of medicines, it is because we continue to treat old age instead of understanding and embracing it. High blood pressure and sugar levels, sore joints, and other age-related conditions are natural processes associated with an old body system. We don't need to be sticking catheters and shunts into so many old heart vessels. Especially when the quality of life is not enhanced or pain significantly reduced, we should just let old people be old and stop nagging them about it.

Even older people who flunked out of a self-help program and abused their health can benefit from the fact that nature is remarkably forgiving. People who once smoked and have stopped have, after five years, no more risk of having a heart attack than those who never smoked.[8] Except for organic disorders such as stroke or Alzheimer's disease that do increase with age, older adults do not show a significant decline in thinking or learning abilities with age.[9] As with their young counterparts, if they stop seeking mental challenges and cease to savor daily life, their mental performance declines.

The comedienne Phyllis Diller lamented, "I'm at the age when my back goes out more than I do." A lot of physical changes occur as we age, and most of what we feel are symptoms, but not of "age disease"; they are symptoms that we are alive and still going strong enough to hurt.

After living among hundreds of dreadfully sick patients, I am convinced that if you have reached the age of seventy, whatever you have been doing is working well and you should keep doing it. Unless you have a specific problem, tell doctors to leave you alone. If a doctor does want to do something to you or tells you to start taking a drug, immediately seek another opinion from an expert on healthy aging, preferably from someone older than eighty who has proven credentials in savoring senior living.

If you're older than seventy, stop worrying about health food. Your diet got you this far, so changing it now is an unnecessary risk. The author Robert Orben was right when he noted, "Old people should not eat health food. They need all the preservatives they can get." The most debilitating physical health problems associated with aging can be reduced, postponed, and even reversed by moderate, regular exercise and the simple commonsense use of my version of a creative self-help program, the SWELMM formula: Stop Worrying, Eat Less, Move More. For older people, I would also add: Indulge Yourself. If you can't indulge yourself when you're old, when can you?

Old age offers us the opportunity to experience a longer "Awe-Full" life, a daily living through which we marvel at the simple magic of ordinary things. Healthy aging relates to the warning from John Henry Cardinal Newman, who wrote, "Fear not that life shall come to an end, but rather that it never had a beginning."

Healthy Dying and Good Grieving

All interest in disease and death is only
another expression of interest in life.

THOMAS MANN

PROPOSITIONS ABOUT DYING AND GRIEVING

1. Death is a creation of human self-consciousness, not a fact of life.
2. Unless we allow them to, people do not "pass away."
3. There are no "stages of grieving and dying."
4. There is no "other side" to which we "cross over."
5. "Nearer-to-life" experiences are more important than "near-death" experiences.

A QUESTION FOR EINSTEIN

In the summer of 1950, a child died. The father wrote that his son's death had shattered "the very structure of [his] existence" and that his

life had "become an almost meaningless void." In a desperate attempt
to find meaning in the cruel finality of death, he wrote to Albert Einstein and asked him whether the brilliant scientist could say something
that might "assuage the pain of an unquenchable longing, an intense
craving, an unceasing love for my darling son."[1]

The grieving father had just read Einstein's *The World As I See It*, in
which the scientist wrote, "Any individual who should survive his physical death is beyond my comprehension . . . such notions are for the
fears or absurd egoism of feeble souls."[2] Coming from the mind of one
of the world's greatest thinkers, these words dashed any hope the an-
guished man had of finding meaning in his son's death. He wrote to
Einstein, "Am I to believe that my beautiful darling child has been forever wedded into dust, that there was nothing within him which has
defied the grave and transcended the power of death?"

This father's pain is known to all of us. Most people have experienced the terrible finality of the loss of a loved one, and some have
faced their own impending deaths. They have sought any source of
comfort from meaning in death, and when I was dangerously ill, my
wife and I engaged in that same search. Although many people hold in-
stitutionalized religious views that offer them comfort, some feel the
need for understanding death beyond an established religion's traditional concepts. However we find comfort, research shows that those
who are able to find meaning after loss or other trauma have lower levels of depression, anxiety, and stress. They also have stronger immune
systems and increased longevity.

Albert Einstein took the time to respond personally to the despon-
dent father, and his words are an example of a mindful approach to the
issue of death. His answer challenges the illusion of the separate self
that is at the core of self-helpism.

This is what Einstein wrote to the grieving father: "A human being is
part of the whole world, called by us 'Universe,' a part of limited time
and space." He went on to say that thinking of ourselves as in any way

separate from that universe and/or walled off from the other persons and things composing that universe is a "kind of optical delusion" of self-consciousness. He added that "striving to free oneself from this delusion is the one issue of true religion," a message quite the opposite of the religion of the holy self.

Einstein advised the mourning father to try to overcome his view of a separate existence for himself, his son, or any being as "the way to reach the attainable measure of peace of mind." His use of the word "attainable" hints at the idea that our search for meaning and benefit in loss has its limits. It is not so much the answer we find but the search that is important, and Einstein's advice to consider the view of infinite connection and the self as an illusion can be helpful in that search.

WHAT DOES DYING MEAN AND
WHAT'S THE BENEFIT?

In 1998, researchers at the University of Michigan conducted a study of people coping with the loss of a family member.[3] By interviewing people whose family members were terminally ill about three months before the family member died and roughly eighteen months after the loss, the researchers discovered something interesting about the nature of meaning that relates to the mindful approach to creative self-help.

We all know that finding meaning is important, but that it can mean different things to different people. The University of Michigan study showed that there were two major understandings of "meaning" in death. (You can see them in the grieving father's letter to Einstein.) One is "making sense" of the event, and the other is actually finding a benefit in the experience.

"Finding a benefit" in the death of a loved one may at first be an appalling thing. But many of us who have cared for a sick relative, or survived the grief of death, can attest to unexpected rewards. The knowledge that a loved one has been released from suffering, the deep empathy and caring poured out by friends and strangers, and the patience, strength, and connection to be found in living with someone close to death are all benefits to be savored.

In the Michigan study, the positive effects of finding meaning were reduced about a year after the loss, but being able to construe some *benefit* from it led to a more stable adjustment eighteen months after the death. The findings from this study remained statistically significant even when the experimenters factored in the subjects' emotional status before the loss, their general levels of optimism and pessimism, their religious beliefs, and the ages of the lost loved ones.

This extraordinary study shed new light on the value of "immediate grief counseling." It indicated the importance of avoiding quick mental closure, or acquiescing too quickly at a vulnerable time to someone else's ideas about the meaning of life and death.

I observed a "grief counselor" speaking to a group of high school students who had lost four of their classmates when a drunk driver smashed into the side of their car. She told the students that they must remember that "everything happens for a reason," but her well-intended advice was probably not helpful because it provided the meaning that healthy grievers must mindfully seek for themselves. It may have been *her* meaning, but because it biased the students' own mindfulness by supplying a ready-made meaning, its long-term value must be questioned.

There probably *is* no reason when such senseless tragedy happens, at least not one that we can ever figure out. We have to remain for a while in a state of irrational suffering and bear the unfairness of life.

SELF-HELP'S WORST FEAR

Experts promise that if we think the right way, we can be physically ageless and never have to die. On one of their iconoclastic shows on cable television (irreverently called *Bullshit*), the magicians Penn and

Teller were examining the self-help movement. They interviewed a self-proclaimed "expert on eternal life" who was leading seminars that promised the ultimate self-help reward, a self that never dies. He said that we die only if we think we can and that not thinking about death defeats it. Penn repeated the title of their show.

Even if we tried such an absurd "help your self never to lose your self" approach, we couldn't succeed at not thinking about death. The psychologist Daniel Wegner wrote a fascinating book, *White Bears and Other Unwanted Things,* in which he describes what scientists call the "ironic process theory."[4] This theory explains why the harder we try not to think of something, the more we do think about it.

Try one of Wegner's experiments yourself. In a few moments, put this book down and sit thinking about anything you want, just not white bears. Don't think about polar bears, the Arctic, snow, or anything to do with white bears. Put the book down and try it for a few minutes.

So how did you do? It's ironic that the very thing I asked you not to think about and that you'd probably never given a lot of thought to until I mentioned it began to take up a lot of space on the hard drive of your consciousness whether you wanted it there or not. That's why it's called the ironic process theory, and it makes an important point about self-help's mind-over-matter approach.

Wegner says that the mind uses two complementary processes to think. One he calls the "intentional operating process" that helps us consciously think about what we want to think about. While this process is at work, however, the "ironic monitoring process" is operating in our unconsciousness. This process is designed to help us avoid thoughts we don't want. When you tried not to think about a white bear, you used your intentional operating process, but your "ironic" process was also looking for thoughts that even remotely resembled white bears so that you could skip over them. The problem is that this very monitoring system makes it virtually impossible not to have the thought you were intentionally trying to avoid.

This science of the mind goes a long way toward explaining why death so preoccupies those who most wish to deny it. We are afraid of death, we shut our eyes to death, we work to prevent or even eliminate it—yet death continually stalks us. The more we pretend it isn't there, the more persistent its presence is in our minds. The only way to over-come our obsession with death, then, is to embrace it.

THERE WAS AN ELEPHANT IN MY ROOM

It's a lucky thing I had Einstein's words to help me when I thought I was dying, because most people around me didn't want anything to do with the topic of death. I suffered from the same *thanatophobia*—fear of dying—that most of us experience. I viewed death as the opposite of life; I saw it either as a horrendously frightening end or as a peaceful transitioning into an afterlife where the separate self continued to exist in some angelic form still distinguishable from all other selves.

Although those who cared for me seemed uncomfortable about discussing it, the specter of death always loomed over the cancer unit. Of course, it does for all of us everywhere, but living where death happens so regularly brings it into the consciousness. Maybe that's why so many cancer patients begin to adopt such a self-less view of living and dying.

For me and the other cancer patients, death was the elephant in the room that everyone knew was there but agreed to pretend not to see. No one knew what to do about it anyway other than provide rote reli-gious explanations or stained-glass platitudes, most often the infamous "everything happens for a reason."

∽

Some of the patients I met with took comfort from authors who claimed to have tapped into their mystic potential to speak regularly with the true death experts, dead people who were now "living," in some way, somewhere on "the other side" of this life. Self-proclaimed psychics claimed to talk directly with one of the billions upon billions of separate selves waiting to be contacted. For some reason, these postlife continuations of Earth-bound separate selves are able to speak only through a "thano-translator." Other patients on my cancer unit sought the wisdom of authors who dispensed with intermediaries and claimed to have conversations directly with God.

Whenever I was able to point to the elephant and ask, "Am I dying?" the answer would be something like "We're all dying" or "Let's not even think about that now" or "Be optimistic and think positively." When these people thought would be a *better* time to think about dying than when I was at death's door was not clear, but they were the ones who were not ready to deal with death. Their medical training had taught them that death was an enemy and a sign of failure. In fact, I learned more about death and dying from a bird outside my window.

CLAUDIA'S GENTLE DEATH

My hospital room window looked out over several trees. I could watch the birds for hours and was eventually able to recognize and give names to individual birds. One bird had caught my eye because it seemed to be in such bad condition and looked as I often felt—weak, trapped, and helpless. I decided to name her Claudia.

One of Claudia's legs was missing, so she had to hop awkwardly after the crumbs tossed by hospital workers on their break. The other birds regularly bullied her, but she didn't seem to take it personally. One of her wings was tucked in such a way that it must have been broken. Claudia could barely fly and I assumed it must have been painful when she tried. She always landed unsteadily and then struggled like a novice tightrope walker trying to find her balance. The more I watched her, the more mindful I became and the more I realized that nature had little concern about the issue that we dreaded the most, the end of the self or the self of someone we love.

I worried each time Claudia tried to move from one branch to another. She would often be jostled off her branch by a breeze or by other birds' hurried comings and goings. She would desperately flap her one good wing, but she would still eventually fall helplessly to the ground and be still for minutes as if she were dead. Then, suddenly, Claudia would quiver, hop, and wobble slowly to shelter, and there she would remain, quivering, for hours. But whenever I checked back to see whether she had moved, she had gone.

Early one evening, I saw Claudia die. The sun was setting, so the black branch on which she was perched stood out in stark contrast against the peaceful orange dusk. There was no breeze at all that evening. As if a ritual were in progress, the other birds were strangely silent.

I wondered whether Claudia had selected that branch and that time to die. She was trembling and seemed to be just barely able to breathe and to hold her place on her branch. She sat for more than two hours on her perch, and finally the evening grew so dark that I could barely see her profile. She had stared out toward the sunset for all those hours, but now she bent and tilted her head to her chest, became very still, and then tumbled to the ground.

At the moment of Claudia's passing, I began to understand why death is such a mysterious, fearful, and difficult concept for we humans. We approach it with fear because we believe in the primacy of the separate self, the illusion of personal power and total control over our destiny, and the belief that our "self" is somehow separate from other selves and the world. Contrary to nature's laws, we believe in, defend, and keep establishing boundaries.

I rang for a nurse and asked whether someone would go out and look for and bury Claudia. I was crying, so the nurse accommodated what

I'm sure she thought was a medication-related psychosis or sign of depression, but I felt energized by this sad moment. I pleaded with the nurse to take me seriously and she reluctantly agreed to put on her jacket and look for Claudia. Although she shook her head in disbelief when she left my room, I saw her take an empty medication box and spoon from a tray as she went to the elevator.

I tried to see what was happening beneath my window, but it was too dark. When the nurse returned to my room, she told me that she had looked everywhere and there was no dead bird to be found. I asked her to look again when she left work and she agreed. I thought she might just be humoring me, but I hoped I was wrong.

The next evening, my nurse returned for her late shift. I asked whether she had looked again when she had left and she said she had. She said she had even looked again when she arrived back at work. "I guarantee you," she said, "there is absolutely no dead bird out there. Maybe it got better. Maybe it didn't really die after all and just flew to another place." I remember thinking that in some important and mysterious way, she was right.

THE DEATH DELUSION

Death is an invention to the mind, the kind that Einstein called an "optical delusion" of consciousness. It is a way of thinking about life that cherishes the idea of an all-powerful separate self, and depends on that idea as the ultimate source of happiness. It is based on the existence of boundaries that nature teaches us every day do not exist. Although there is pain and dying for all living things, these events are not the big deal for nature that we humans make of them.

I know that when someone accidentally steps on my golden retriever Lia's tail, she yelps, forgets it, turns over, and goes back to sleep. Perhaps because she is living in dog years, she is not bothered about having only ten or so human years left to live. I know that whenever we have had to have one of our old dogs "put to sleep," our family has agonized through the process, but our dogs showed a resigned calmness. They weren't consumed with themselves, but we were.

We might assume that animals' disregard of the seriousness of death happens because they're stupid, and that our narrow genetic percentage of difference from some of them renders us smart; but who is really wiser when it comes to the issue of time passing and lives ending? Although I can't really know, Claudia didn't seem to spend much of her bird life worrying about dying, thinking about her "self," or seeking her identity. I don't think she attended bird motivational seminars or went on low-carb birdseed diets. She always seemed too urgently involved in leading her own good life to worry about or strive for a better one. I doubt she even thought there was one to be had.

We humans work like dogs, but maybe we would benefit from thinking a little more like them when it comes to the assumed boundary between life and death. Nature's way of barrier-free thinking holds lessons for us about transcending our perspective on life. The starting point for rethinking the ideas of self-help is to think slowly and long about death, what it will mean to us, and what benefits its reality might hold.

When I was ill, I often thought about how much my family loved me and I began to sense that in many ways my fear of dying was a reflection of my selfishness. When I saw the tears in the eyes of a patient who had been told by a medium that his deceased father had sent a message of love, I was skeptical; but I thought, if the message has meaning for this person, who am I to judge? Maybe the medium's speaking for the patient's father confirmed for the patient that he would, after all, live forever in the memories and hearts of his loved ones. As is true of all those who earn our deepest love, his mortality rested in his loving connection with his family, not in his individual existence someplace where only a medium is allowed to make contact. I thought then that the words of the author Thomas Campbell expressed what I was thinking. He wrote, "To live in the hearts we leave behind, is not to die."

NOTES ON NARCISSISM

If we think of the "self" as an individual physical existence and consciousness, that self does eventually die. If we think we are a separate bag of cells under the command of a brain separate from all other brains, we're doomed. But if we are mindful of Albert Einstein's reference to the self as an "optical illusion," that self becomes a figment of the imagination and a symptom of the persistent egocentrism that is fed by the self-help culture.

We have yet to grasp the idea that *losing* one's sense of self, not enhancing and protecting it, is the ultimate path to daily joy and immortality. Most of us have yet to learn Claudia's lesson of local pain in the context of cosmic joy. "I" ends, but "we" don't.

Throughout this book, I have been critical of the narcissism that underlies the personal power, enhanced self-esteem, and self-potentialism movements. I have discussed how it contributes to our elevation of death to enemy status and how we spend our lives uselessly and needlessly fighting it. Mindfulness, however, guarantees that nothing is ever simple or one-sided. The more my own mindfulness about narcissism led me to despise narcissism as a form of arrogant selfishness, the more it also led me to realize that hating a syndrome that has its origins in the lack of love made little sense. It was then that I came to see narcissism as a social problem manifested through individual selfishness.

A pharmacist may have developed Tono-Bungay, but the unquestioned acceptance and mass dependence it commanded were symptoms of the gullibility of a mindlessly self-enhancing society. I no longer think that narcissism alone is the problem; it's the narcissism we practice and which the self-help movement promulgates that leads us in the wrong direction.

As I was writing this chapter, I came upon my old notes from my courses in psychoanalysis. I had written that there are two kinds of narcissism. Primary narcissism resembles the innocent self-love shown by very young children; this type of narcissism causes youngsters to behave as if they were oblivious to anyone but themselves. It's not that children are *selfish*, but that, like Claudia, they don't think about the idea of "self." They just "are."

The narcissism that concerned me then, as now, is "secondary narcissism." This form of self-absorption is at the core of self-helpism, at the root of our thanataphobia, and a reason why years of self-helping still haven't led most of us to the happiness the guides to the good life promise.

Secondary narcissism is much less spontaneous than primary narcissism; it's a matter of elective, egotistical self-regard, not true concern for others. It means becoming intentionally consumed with the self and trying to become even *more* self-aware and self-loving—not just being carried away by the irresistible joy of being alive. Primary narcissists' innocent savoring of life inevitably draws others to them to help them discover the joy of connection that ultimately overwhelms their independent delight. On the other hand, secondary narcissists' self-focus leaves them abandoned and alone on the path to finding the fulfilled but separate self.

THE MAGIC OF MEMORIES

Think back now to memories of a deceased loved one. I promise you that they are not repressed but just waiting for your attention. You will find that your brain has almost totally forgotten the features of the person it was most interested in. One of the most frustrating and saddening aspects of losing someone dear to us is that we feel we can't ever see, touch, or hear that person again. Even if we have videotapes, we see only ghosts and images, not the person we loved. Try as you might, you will not be able to see a clear image of the person's face or hear the voice as it was when that person was alive. But you will, if you put your consciousness to it, be able to recall *his* or *her* consciousness, that representation of the person that wasn't a separate self but an intimate part of you. You will sense beyond words how the remembered one was, how you loved each other. That's how our nonlocal, time- and space-free consciousness works. If it exists, that may be where immortality ultimately resides.

Human instinct has an immense capacity for seeing to it that we survive, but it has become so severely nearsighted (or perhaps more descriptively "me-optic") that it is almost useless for helping us thrive. The brain's dread of losing itself and its body is interfering with the mindful learning about the seven areas of life you have read about. Perhaps because death is the archenemy of the ever-enhanced self, the brain's ironic monitoring system is designed to see that we will sooner or later pay attention to the lessons it offers us about living.

Our thanatophobia is reflected in Hollywood's bizarre horror movies: charlatans speaking for those "from the other side," cloning, cryonics, and fencing off graveyards as far from view as possible. I learned from my illness that the assumption of a clear and distinct boundary between life and death is what makes dying so difficult and death so beyond the comprehension of the selfish human brain.

WATER LOGIC

Our boundary consciousness serves to solidify the illusory barriers not only between us as people but between a whole life and ourselves. This is the kind of thinking that is at the root of the self-help movement; despite its proclamation of unconditional love of everything and everyone, it really focuses on self-adoration, representation, and enhancement.

The physician and psychologist Edward de Bono calls this kind of thinking "rock logic," which he contrasts with a more selfless and connective "water logic."[5] If we see ourselves as a separate rock, even when we join up with another rock, we still end up being two rocks. Water logic does not acknowledge boundaries or separateness. If we think of ourselves as water and merge with another person, water plus water is still water. As a wise Hawaiian friend of mine said, "Always remember, even during the stormiest times of life, we are all waves in the ocean of life flowing forever together."

Lost in all the glitz and glitter of psychic mediums and claims about near-death experiences, ghosts, and other products of the thanatophobia industry is the sound research of a humble scientist who offers evidence worth our attention regarding the "barrier" between life and death. His work illustrates the "water logic" or oceanic thinking of the unselfish Hawaiian culture in which I live.

TIMELESS SOULS

Ian Stevenson is a professor of psychology at the University of Virginia. For thirty-seven years, he has traveled to Lebanon, India, and the southern United States investigating and meticulously documenting more than 2,000 stories of young children who say they have had previous lives.[6] Many more people know and trust famous television psychics than know of Dr. Stevenson and his highly respected scientific work. But that work is much more impressive, more startling in its implications, and more instructive about the issues of death and dying than the performances of the star-status mediums.

Stevenson's cases suggest the absence of a boundary between life and death. When Tom Shroder, the skeptical editor of the *Washington Post*'s Sunday "Style" section, accompanied Stevenson to observe his cases firsthand, he reported that he could not discount them. Thousands of young children described specific details of families they said were their own in their former lives. Unlike prior popular reports about reincarnation, these accounts were not induced by hypnosis or accounts of life led centuries ago. They were accounts of real families, in the present, but living in other towns and countries, from children who recalled that before their deaths, they had lived with these families. When the families met as total strangers brought together by a scientist tracking down a child's memory of another life, the verification of the details of the child's reports were remarkable. In some cases, birthmarks on the child recalling a prior life corresponded perfectly with injuries that had killed the person the child believed he had been in a previous life.

I highly recommend that you read Dr. Stevenson's work. He hasn't been on Oprah, Dr. Phil, or other talk shows. He does not consider himself a medium, he is not entirely sure what his research means, and he does not provide on-air psychic readings or communications with the dead. He doesn't offer a self-help guide to reincarnation, nor does he assert that it even exists. He is a scientist asking questions about the possibility that the boundary we think exists between life and death and the past, now, and the future may not exist other than as a way to think about life that allows us to bring order to our lives.

FIVE PROPOSITIONS ABOUT DYING

My own experience as a person facing death, and my family's experience as they prepared to face it with me, has helped me in conceiving of a healthy, mindful way of thinking about dying and grieving. Here are my propositions on death:

Death Proposition Number One: Death is a creation of human self-consciousness, not a fact of life.   As you have read, unless we think of boundaries and of the "self" as exclusively an individual body and separate consciousness, death as a permanent end is *not* a fact of life. If we use water logic instead of rock logic, we fully savor our opportunities to connect with others and make ourselves available for their lasting love. Loving relationships are far more than physical, so they can transcend physical ending. An indelible love imprint is left on the consciousness of those who have realized that loving and familying is the way we transcend the fear of death.

If we have already given ourselves away, we don't have a self that can be taken, not even by death. If our thinking allows it, the self can become immersed within a connective system where death does not exist. If we seek immortality, our efforts should be aimed at nurturing a lasting love, not going to the spiritual in-betweens who call themselves mediums. By loving totally and abandoning the myth of self-potential, we forge shared memories that resonate forever in the hearts of those who made them.

Death Proposition Number Two: Unless we allow them to, people do not "pass away."   When I was ill, I spent hours scanning my memories for the images, voices, and smells of the people I had loved who had died. I had never taken that much time to search my consciousness for the memory of loving relationships from my past. Until a crisis intervened, I had usually been busier doing than remembering and had carelessly and foolishly squandered time I could have spent savoring memories of those I loved. They hadn't passed away; I had allowed them to pass too far from my consciousness. They were there all along just waiting for me to remember them.

After terrible sickness focused my attention on how I lived, I took much more time and paid much more attention not only to my memories but to the quality of new experiences that will become memories. I now look more deeply at the faces of those I love and who love me so that I can be sure a loving imprint is constantly being painted in my memory. I pay more attention to how I live and love so that I may become worthy of being a powerfully indelible loving memory easily accessible to those I hope will always remember me.

With death happening all around me, I began to think about my deceased father not as a separate being but as emotions resonating in my heart and recollections etched in my soul. When I stopped looking outside and up and began to look in, I was finally able to find him and I could see him more clearly than I ever had since his death so many years ago. I could hear him speaking to me in wordless messages. Mindfulness often leaves me speechless.

Memories I had about my father came to my consciousness much as Hawaiian rainbows appear from nowhere, disappear, and then reappear. When I told my mother about these memories, she said I would have been much too young to have them, but that I was accurate, down to the last detail.

Death Proposition Number Three: There are no "stages of grieving and dying."   Perhaps because of its fixation on the importance of the separate self, the self-help movement has long been involved with the issue of dying and grieving. It makes what one calls "the grief work assumption."[7] "Grief work" or "working through" emotions associated with grief is thought to be the best way to help someone deal with death, but research shows this is not always so.

Recent studies of grief counseling have not only failed to support the helpfulness of the "grief work and working through" approach to loss, they have shown that grief counselors may also be doing unintentional harm to those in the process of bereavement by imposing emotions and thoughts that would not otherwise occur or engendering guilt for not having the right emotion at the right time. Studies show that most grieving people don't need such intervention.[8] Most of us do not experience prolonged distress or depression following the death of a loved one. This does not mean that we had a superficial attachment to the person we lost; it means that because we were given life, we were also given the means to deal with its end. Most of us are capable of dealing with transitional life crises without intervention. Most of us pass through the bereavement process and learn and grow from it, but the pathogenic orientation of the self-help movement persists in trying to "treat" this process.

According to the "grief work" assumption, grieving is supposed to involve long and deeply felt sadness experienced and shown through certain stages, but again, research does not verify that most of us grieve in that way. Despite the excruciating pain of loss, most of us are naturally resilient enough to suffer terribly for a while and then move on. This resilience does not mean that we are "in denial"; but if we are, so what? It means we are made to live, to celebrate, to suffer, to die, to grieve, and to become more alive. As Einstein told the grieving father, resilience means we are conscious beings for whom all life's challenges become part of our memories and the nature of our character.

Death Proposition Number Four: There is no "other side" to which we "cross over."   Perhaps we need to think of death as taking us to "another side" because we are afraid of the idea that there is only one side, one infinite whole, and that we're "in it" right now and not living to qualify for "up there" later. We aren't rehearsing. This is it!

I never felt closer to my deceased father than when I realized I didn't have to try to "contact" him from somewhere else or to hire someone to find him for me. If I opened my mind and heart, I could easily communicate with him. I did not feel that he was somewhere else or on another side. Unless I constructed the barrier, his physical absence didn't place him over it. He was with me then, right here.

When I was ill, one of my Hawaiian teachers spoke to me about the illusion of modern society's kind of death. He had come to visit me just after Claudia died. I was crying again about it and told him what I had observed. With his typical combination of wisdom and humor, he said, "Well, it doesn't sound like Claudia or her bird friends were nearly as upset about it as you are."

"You see," said the *kahuna*, "death is not a rock wall barrier between one life and our hope for another. We are not just part of a whole, we are the whole. Think of the wave that is childishly afraid that it will end when it breaks upon the shore. It doesn't need to be frightened. It is the ocean. It cannot break and cannot end. When it thinks of itself as separate from the ocean, that's when it suffers and becomes needlessly afraid. That's when it fails to feel the thrill and joy of being the ocean. Always remember the lesson of the wave. Remember when you are afraid of ending that nothing ever ends. Even if you think like a rock, you're still a wave and you are the ocean."

As I reflected on the wisdom of the *kahuna's* words, I thought again about how Claudia had died. She had shown no understanding or concern for herself as a separate thing. The other birds had appeared to show respect for the transition she was experiencing, but they showed no fear. Everything happened just as it should and all the birds seem to know, and in some way understand.

I thought how much of life we spend in a fear of death that is fueled by the illusion of a separate self. I thought how silly that was because the best of times happen when we are unaware of ourselves. Worrying about the end of ourselves makes us fail to be fully alive. I know now that although our worries about the pain and suffering of death are understandable, our fear of dying is without merit.

Death Proposition Number Five: "Nearer-to-life" experiences are more important than "near-death" experiences.   One of the most popular self-help myths about death is the "near-death experience." Because my illness was so severe that my vital signs dropped below a life-sustaining level more than once, I am frequently asked whether I had a near-death experience. Apparently, there's a dying program we're supposed to follow. It usually includes some form of movement or floating sensation, of passing through a tunnel toward a light radiating invitingly from "the other side," and of encountering deceased loved ones or a

God-like figure. When I joke that this description sounds less like passing to the other side than emerging from inside one's mother in the birth process, my questioners think I am being sacrilegious.

I know for sure that I nearly died, but I don't know whether I had a near-death experience. Maybe I was too afraid to recognize it. Sometimes I think I did have an experience similar to those described above, but I also know that I knew about them before I faced death and may have been experiencing a self-fulfilling prophecy. I am probably re-creating now what I thought I must or should have experienced when I was near death. Maybe I was glimpsing some divine mystery; or more likely, I experienced a dying brain and the biochemical changes taking place within it. I just don't know. But I do know that thinking about these things helps me learn more about the meaning of life and how to cherish it.

As a neuropsychologist, I also know that a dying brain lacks oxygen and that this condition can lead to all sorts of delusions. I know that an extremely rapid heartbeat can produce excessive carbon dioxide, which could result in hallucinations, dizziness, and the sense of floating. I don't know whether these issues are necessarily at the core of the "near-death experience," but I do think that the near-death experience is just another attempt to answer Job's question: "If a man shall die, shall he live again?"

I have thought hard about my answer to Job's question. And my answer is no. I don't think we will live "again" with a beating heart and an alert brain, or in some ethereal form occasionally called forth by a medium fluent in death-speak. I've come to think that it doesn't matter. What *does* matter is to realize that fearing death deprives us of being fully alive and, like most fears, is most likely irrational.

As Socrates reflected, "To fear death is nothing other than to think oneself wise when one is not, for it is to think one knows what one does not know." That's the view that my mindfulness about death and dying has led me to believe. We just don't know what the manifestation of consciousness will be when we experience physical end, but our consciousness is encouraging us to be more mindful of the infinite possibilities of the human spirit. I've come to believe that the more fully mindful we are of life as it is infinitely entwined with other lives, the more we realize that there is an aspect of immortality that we can influence right now.

Maybe a little selfishness is defensible if it derives from trying to live and love to assure a permanent loving residence in the hearts of others. I know that, at least for me, Claudia is immortal in my memory because of the fearless and gentle way she died. She may not have been capable of knowing her "self," but nonetheless she helped me. She taught me that death is the end of the self as we know it—and that such a way of knowing should have died long ago.

The Fifth Factor

May the story give you strength.
May the belief relieve your pain.

MOHAWK INDIAN HEALER

THE BIG FIVE

In the 1970s, research psychologists summarized the studies on mental and physical health. They identified what came to be called "The Big Five" personality traits most likely to lead to a sense of well-being.[1] There's no mention in this research of the value of enhancing self-esteem, being all we can be, never having guilt, or suffering inner children. Instead, the data show that non-self-focused behaviors are crucial to a good and long life. The Big Five are:

- Extroversion: Reaching out to others is healthier than focusing on yourself.

- Agreeableness: Being compliant and pleasant is healthier than being assertive and self-representing.
- Emotional Stability: Monitoring and controlling our emotions is healthier than "letting them all out."
- Openness: Being open and vulnerable with and toward others is healthier than constantly trying to exert personal power or enhance our own self-esteem.
- Conscientiousness: Being cognizant of what others think and intentionally trying to live up to others' expectations is healthier than the constant pursuit of selfish goals.

SELF-CONSCIOUS OR
SELFLESSLY CONSCIENTIOUS?

The fifth of the above "Big Five" personality factors is conscientiousness, defined as a propensity toward impulse control, responsibility, orderliness, and compliance. Conscientiousness is primarily "us" consciousness. The researcher Brent Roberts said that it is "related to every single reason why we die young." His data show that those of us who are the most conscientious and socially compliant are also most likely to live the longest and happiest, yet self-helpism tends to focus almost exclusively on "self" consciousness rather than on community well-being.[2]

One of the early fathers of the self-help and personal potential movement was the therapist Fritz Perls. He was a staunch opponent of trying to lead life by the Fifth Factor of trying to please others, to fit in, and to go humbly along trying to share a savored life with those around us. He told his followers, "Your rights end where my nose begins." Perls was a leader in the Gestalt psychology movement, which predates modern self-helpism. He was one of the first to articulate the "do your own thing" philosophy that underlies it. Although the German word *gestalt* refers to a whole or a pattern that is more than the sum of its parts, Perls's version of becoming whole was to assert one small part of the collective whole, the fully actualized self. For Perls and his colleagues, the Fifth Factor was a limiting influence that was at best placed a distant second to expressing oneself fully, regardless of what others think and feel.

FAUX PERLS

Along with other self-help pioneers such as Carl Rogers, Rollo May, and Abraham Maslow, Perls assumed not only that we are all less than we can be but that the weaknesses and strengths of an individual reside exclusively within, and not between. Concern for others was given a glancing nod. At the top of the pyramid of well-being sat "self-actualization."

I observed a psychologist who was trained by Fritz Perls as he led a Gestalt therapy group session. When a woman in the group said she spent a lot of time worrying about what others thought about her, the rest of the group shook their heads in disbelief, and the therapist immediately jumped to his feet. He went directly to her face and yelled, "Grow up, for God's sake! You're not still a dependent little girl seeking Mommy's approval, are you? Where's your self-respect? You'll never find it by going along or trying to prove that you're a nice and love-worthy person. You are already love-worthy, you don't have to earn it. For God's sake, woman, have you not been listening all these weeks? Start looking into yourself and doing your own thing." As she promised to start doing the therapist's and group's thing, the woman broke into tears. When she said she finally felt free of the burden of "being so damned selfless," the group gathered with the therapist to give her what the psychologist said was "a group hug to squeeze her self back inside where it belongs instead of limping around outside looking for approval." Apparently, seeking the approval of the group and the therapist was acceptable.

Because of the influence of Gestalt Psychology and its many versions, psychotherapy and pop psychology advice became based on helping individuals get in touch with their inner selves and then freeing that newly discovered individual of such life-limiting ideas as obligation, duty, responsibility, deference, and concern for others. The ultimate failure was not related to our interactions with others, but our failure to work harder to be all we can be.

"MUSTURBATION" AND "SHOULD-ING" ON YOURSELF

According to Perls's view and much of today's popular psychology, doing something out of a sense of responsibility is "musturbation," an antecedent of the dreaded codependence. His group therapy programs focused on each individual's purging herself of a sense of obligation, which he called "should-ing" on oneself. The Gestalt therapist whose group I observed told a group member, "You think about what you should do to please others. Should, should, should. You're going to continue to lead your crappy life if you don't stop should-ing all over yourself." The group laughed as the patient blushed.

Perls's emphasis on personal power and self-fulfillment above all continues today in the form of the narcissistic psycho-philosophy of self-helpism I have attempted to debunk in this book. We cannot be sure whether he and his modern-day counterparts are the cause or effect of the "me first" consciousness, but it still seems to exert influence in our national psyche.

TWO PRAYERS

As evidence of the religious nature of self-helpism, Fritz Perls offered what he called his "Gestalt therapy prayer."[3] Perls's "prayer for the free and fulfilled self" clearly expresses the individualism that is the core belief of all practicing self-potentialists. As a conclusion to this book, I offer it here along with the contrarian responses to it that I wrote several years ago as I reviewed the results of my study of Gestalt therapy.

Perls:

I do my thing, and you do your thing.

> But maybe, if you just do your thing and I do mine,
> We risk losing each other and the memories we can make together
> forever.

Perls:

I am not in this world to live up to your expectations,

> But maybe I am in this world to try to live up to what you need from
> me, to help you fulfill your expectations, and by doing so I learn
> about the joy of loving connection.

Perls:

And you are not in this world to life up to mine.

> But maybe, you are also in this world to do your best to be mindful
> of how I think, what I feel, and to try to live up to my expectations.

Perls:

You are you and I am I,

> But maybe, there is no true distinction between "you" and "I" other
> than the one we create in our own consciousness.

Perls:

And if by chance we find each other, it's beautiful.

> But maybe finding each other is a matter of intentional choice, per-
> sistent effort, and commitment that, when lacking, makes life seem
> less beautiful.

Perls:

If not, it can't be helped.

> But maybe, because we are capable of being mindful of all that we
> do and feel, we can choose to put one another before ourselves, and
> that always helps everyone and, ultimately, the world.

I hope my answer to Fritz Perls's prayer offers you and those you love some different "pearls" of wisdom about "the good life." I hope it will serve as a "re-minder" for you to consider self-help advice from a contrarian point of view. If, in these increasingly turbulent and disconnected times, we don't think more mindfully about the pervasive influence of self-helpism, heaven help us.

Notes

Introduction. A Science of Well-Being

1. When adversity strikes, we need a way to explain and deal with what is happening to us. We need to develop our "explanatory style" and create our own sense of what psychologists call "coherence." Pioneering work on the concept of coherences can be found in A. Antonovsky, *Unraveling the Mystery of Health: How People Manage Stress and Stay Well* (San Francisco: Jossey-Bass, 1987).

2. For a description of this classic study, see C. L. M. Keyes and J. Haidt, "Complete Mental Health: An Agenda for the 21st Century," in *Flourishing: Positive Psychology and the Life Well Lived,* ed. C. L. M. Keyes and J. Haidt (Washington, D.C.: American Psychological Association, 2003), 293–312.

Chapter 1. Self-Help Needs Our Help

1. Reported by Joan Patterson in the *Las Vegas-Review Journal,* 1998; see http://www.reviewjournral.com/lvrj_home/1998/Feb–24-Tue–1998/lifestyles/6989890.htm.

2. S. Smiles and P. W. Sinneman, eds., *Self-Help* (New York: Oxford University Press, 2002), 5.

3. Ibid., 6.

4. P. P. Quimby, *The Complete Writings,* vols. 1, 2, and 3 (New York: DeVorss, 1988).

5. H. W. Dresser, ed., *Quimby Manuscripts 1921* (New York: Kessinger, 2003).

6. N. V. Peale, *The Power of Positive Thinking* (New York: Random House, 1992).

7. H. Smith, "Beyond the Post-Modern Mind," interview by Jeffrey Mishlove, *Thinking Out Loud Productions*, 1998, http://www.intuition.org/txt/smith.htm.

8. A description of this study can be found at http://www.age-of-the-sage.org/psychology/milgram_obedience_experiment.html.

9. S. Smiles and P. W. Sinmens, *Self Help: Conduct and Perseverance* (London: Oxford University Press, 2002).

10. M. M. Burg and T. E. Seeman, "Families and Health: The Negative Side of Social Ties," *Annals of Behavioral Medicine* 16 (1994): 710–722.

Chapter 2. The Facts of Life?

1. K. E. Stanovich and R. F. West, "Individual Differences in Rational Thought," *Journal of Experimental Psychology* 127, no. 2 (1998): 161–188.

2. D. G. Myers, *Psychology* (New York: Worth, 2004), 20.

3. M. Garry, E. F. Loftus, and S. W. Brown, "Memory: A River Runs Through It," *Consciousness and Cognition* 3 (1994): 438–451.

4. W. Maltz, *The Sexual Healing Journey* (New York: HarperCollins, 1991).

5. E. Loftus, "The Reality of Repressed Memories," *American Psychologist* 48 (1993): 14–22.

6. E. Loftus and K. Ketcham, *The Myth of Repressed Memory* (New York: St. Martin's Press, 1994): 38.

7. E. Loftus and L. Kaufman, "Why Do Traumatic Experiences Sometimes Produce Good Memory (Flashbulbs) and Sometimes No Memory (Repression)?" in *Affect and Accuracy in Recall: Studies of "Flashbulb" Memories*, ed. E. Winograd and U. Neisser (New York: Cambridge University Press, 1992).

8. C. P. Malquist, "Children Who Witness Parental Murder: Post-Traumatic Aspects," *Journal of the American Academy of Child Psychiatry* 25 (1986): 320–325.

9. C. P. Thompson et al., "Involuntary Memories in Depressed and Nondepressed Individuals" (paper presented to the Psychonomic Society Convention, 1996).

10. D. S. Holmes, "Is There Evidence for Repression? No" (unexpurgated version of an article rewritten by the *Harvard Mental Health Letter* and published as "Is There Evidence for Repression? Doubtful") (June 1994): 4–6.

11. W. B. Helmreich, *Against All Odds: Holocaust Survivors and the Successful Lives They Made in America* (New York: Simon & Schuster, 1992).

12. This statement and an excellent summary and presentation of the research on repressed memories and their recovery can be found in S. Brandon et al., "Re-

covered Memories of Childhood Sexual Abuse: Implications for Clinical Practice," *British Journal of Psychiatry* 172 (1998): 294–307.

13. J. W. Dean, *Blind Ambition* (New York: Simon & Schuster, 1976).

14. N. Brandon, "In Defense of 'Self,'" *Association for Humanistic Psychology Perspectives* (August-September 1984): 12–13.

15. R. Dawes, *House of Cards: Psychology and Psychotherapy Built on Myth* (New York: Free Press, 1996): 234.

16. Willard Gaylin, from an interview in *Publishers Weekly*, March 23, 1990.

17. An Australian study of 179 cancer patients was published in the journal *Cancer*. It showed that hope and optimism can be too taxing for some cancer patients, that there is no evidence that it improved the chances of surviving cancer, and that by encouraging hope we can discourage expressions of pessimism that are also legitimate feelings worthy of exploration. See D. Yee, "In Cancer, Bright Side Has Downside," *Honolulu Advertiser*, February 28, 2004, A1 and A5.

18. Ibid., A5.

19. B. Alexander, P. Hadaway, and R. Coambs, "Rat Park Chronicle," in *Illicit Drugs in Canada*, ed. J. Blackwell and P. Eriskson (Toronto University Press, 1999), 565–566.

20. J. Olds and P. Milner, "Positive Reinforcement Produced by Electrical Stimulation of Septal Area and Other Regions of the Rat Brain," *Journal of Comparative and Physiological Psychology* 47 (1954): 419–422.

21. S. Jarvis, *Drug Prevention with Youth* (Tulsa, Okla.: National Resource Center for Youth Services, 1994).

22. For a fascinating description of the work of Bruce Alexander and other researchers whose work should have strongly influenced our thinking about the issues dealt with by self-help, see L. Slater, *Opening Skinner's Box: Great Psychological Experiments of the Twentieth Century* (New York: W. W. Norton, 2004). This quote from Alexander is on page 166.

23. For the best introduction to this topic, see Martin Seligman, *Authentic Happiness: Using the New Positive Psychology to Realize Your Potential for Lasting Fulfillment* (New York: Free Press, 2002). My own book, *The Beethoven Factor: The New Positive Psychology of Hardiness, Happiness, Healing, and Hope* (Charlottesville, Va.: Hampton Roads, 2003), also deals with this new and exciting field of creative self-help.

24. D. Westen, "The Scientific Legacy of Sigmund Freud: Toward a Psychodynamically Informed Psychological Science," *Psychological Bulletin* 124 (1998): 576–577.

Chapter 3. Savoring Your Own Good Life

1. C. L. M. Keyes and C. D. Ryff, "Psychological Well-Being in Midlife," in *Middle Aging: Development in the Third Quarter of Life,* ed. S. L. Willis and J. D. Reid (Orlando, Fla.: Academic Press), 161–180. See also C. L. M. Keyes and S. J. Lopez, "Toward a Science of Mental Health: Positive Directions in Diagnosis and Interventions," in *The Handbook of Positive Psychology,* ed. C. R. Snyder and S. J. Lopez (New York: Oxford University Press, 2002), 45–49.

2. E. Langer, *Mindfulness* (Reading, Mass.: Addison-Wesley, 1989). See also E. Langer's "Well-Being: Mindfulness Versus Positive Evaluation," in *Handbook of Positive Psychology,* ed. C. R. Snyder and S. J. Lopez (New York: Oxford University Press, 2002), 214–230.

3. W. Mischel and N. Baker, "Cognitive Appraisals and Transformations in Delay Behavior," *Journal of Personality and Social Psychology* 31 (1975): 254–261.

4. I took this quote from the *Chronicle of Higher Education,* June 12, 1991, B3.

5. For a discussion of their preliminary work in the new field they are creating called "savoring," see Martin Seligman, *Authentic Happiness: Using the New Positive Psychology to Realize Your Potential for Lasting Fulfillment* (New York: Free Press, 2002), 110.

6. There are several examples of this research. For example, see A. Clarke and A. D. Clarke, *Early Experience: Myth and Evidence* (New York: Free Press, 1976).

7. J. Lusseyran, *And There Was Light* (New York: Parabola Books, 1994).

Chapter 4. Developing a Contrarian Consciousness

1. This and other fascinating examples of counterintuitive facts can be found in T. Gilovich, *How We Know What Isn't So: The Fallibility of Human Reason in Everyday Life* (New York: Free Press, 1991).

2. P. Kurtz, "Stars, Planets, and People," *The Skeptical Inquirer* (Spring 1983): 66.

3. J. Metcalfe and W. Mischel, "A Hot/Cool System Analysis of Delay Gratification: Dynamics of Willpower," *Psychological Review* 106 (1999): 1–6.

4. C. G. Lord, L. Ross, and M. Lepper, "Biased Assimilation and Attitude Polarization: The Effects of Prior Theories on Subsequently Considered Evidence," *Journal of Personality and Social Psychology* 37 (1979): 2098–2109.

5. M. Lepper, C. A. Anderson, and L. Ross, "Perseverance of Social Theories: The Role of Explanation in the Persistence of Discredited Information," *Journal of Personality and Social Psychology* 39 (1980): 1037–1049.

6. D. G. Lord, L. Ross, and M. Lepper, "Considering the Opposite: A Corrective Strategy for Social Judgment," *Journal of Personality and Social Psychology* 47 (1984): 1231–1247.

7. R. Jervis, as quoted in D. Goleman, "Political Forces Come Under New Scrutiny of Psychology," *New York Times*, March 6, 1999, C1 and C4.

8. R. Dawes, *House of Cards: Psychology and Psychotherapy Built on Myth* (New York: Free Press, 1996), 74.

9. In doing the research for this book, I interviewed fifty men and women who were therapists, counselors, coaches, or trainers. Six were licensed psychologists. I gave them the following list of names of researchers who, like those described in this book, had done what most scientists consider to be essentially important work in the field of psychology. I picked ten names that all scientific psychologists should know and that seemed relevant to counseling someone regarding issues of daily living. They were Stanley Milgram (destructive obedience and the myth of the "authoritarian personality"), Solomon Asch, (perceptual distortions), David Rosnehan (errors and biases in clinical judgment), Elizabeth Loftus (the myth of repressed memories), Leon Festinger (cognitive dissonance as it affects our judgment and behavior), Bruce Alexander (myths of the addictive personality), Jerome Kagan (the role of temperament and perspectives on myths about parental influence), Paul Ekman (emotions and facial expressions), Kurt Lewin (ecological psychology and the impact of environment on feelings and behavior), Emmy Werner (psychological resiliency of children), and George Valliant (research on healthy aging and the value of sustained adult relationships to override isolated childhood trauma).

10. Here's my self-help skeptics satire list: J. Bines and G. Greenberg, *Self-Helpless: The Greatest Self-Help Books You'll Never Read* (Franklin Lakes, N.J.: Career Press, 1999); B. S. Held, *Stop Smiling, Start Kvetching: A 5-Step Guide to Creative Complaining* (New York: St. Martin's Griffin, 2001); K. Salmansohn, *How to Be Happy, Dammit: A Cynic's Guide to Spiritual Awareness* (Berkeley, Calif.: Celestial Arts, 2001); K. Salmansohn, *How to Change Your Entire Life by Doing Absolutely Nothing* (New York: Simon & Schuster, 2003); C. C. Schmidtt, *Cosmic Relief* (Houston, Tex.: Brockton Publishing, 2001).

Chapter 5. Love Lies and Why We Believe Them

1. For one example of a careful scientist's view of "L" energy, see the work of Robert G. Jahn, director of the Princeton Engineering Anomalies Research program at Princeton University. He uses the terms "L" and "love energy" in his article "Information, Consciousness, and Health," *Alternative Therapies* 2 (1996): 34.

2. Y. Hu and N. Goldman, "Mortality Differentials by Marital Status: An International Comparison," *Demography* 27 (1990): 233–250.

3. D. G. Myers, *Psychology* (New York: Worth Publishers, 2004), 184.

4. Bureau of the Census, *Statistical Abstract of the United States, 1998* (Washington, D.C.: Government Printing Office), 1998.

5. H. S. Friedman et al., "Psychological and Behavioral Predictors of Longevity: The Aging and Death of the 'Termites,'" *American Psychologist* 50 (1995): 69–78.

6. These data are summarized by the psychologist David Myers in his informative and scientifically based book *The American Paradox: Spiritual Hunger in an Age of Plenty* (New Haven, Conn.: Yale University Press, 2000). This work can serve as an "introductory psychology text" for use in your own self-help program as recommended in Chapter 6.

7. R. Ryan, as quoted by Alfie Kohn, "In Pursuit of Affluence, At a Price," *New York Times,* Feb. 2, 1999, http://www.nytimes.com., 525 and 526.

8. E. Hatfield, "Passionate and Companionate Love," in *The Psychology of Love,* ed. R. J. Sternberg and M. L. Barnes (New Haven, Conn.: Yale University Press, 1988).

9. D. G. Dutton and A. P. Aron, "Some Evidence for Heightened Sexual Attraction Under Conditions of High Anxiety," *Journal of Personality and Social Psychology* 30 (1974): 510–517.

10. G. L. White and D. Knight, "Misattribution of Arousal and Attraction: Effects of Salience of Explanations for Arousal," *Journal of Experimental Social Psychology* 20 (1984): 55–64.

11. E. Berscheid, S. W. Gangestad, and D. Kulakowski, "Emotion in Close Relationships: Implications for Relationship Counseling," in *Handbook of Counseling Psychology,* ed. S. D. Brown and R. W. Lent (New York: Wiley, 1984), 734.

12. G. Downey and S. Feldman, "Implications of Rejection Sensitivity for Intimate Relationships," *Personal Relationships* 7 (1996): 1327–1343.

13. For a summary of the research supporting love's relationship to health and happiness, see D. Ornish, *Love and Survival: The Scientific Basis for the Healing Power of Intimacy* (New York: HarperCollins, 1998).

14. O. Guinness, *The American Hour: A Time of Reckoning and the Once and Future Role of Faith* (New York: Free Press, 1993), 309.

15. J. Bradshaw, *Treating Love: The Last Great Stage of Growth* (New York: Bantam Books, 1992), 342.

16. G. K. Levinger and H. L. Rausch, eds., *Close Relationships: Perspectives on the Meaning of Intimacy* (Boston: University of Massachusetts Press, 1977), 67.

17. B. Gray-Little and N. Burks, "Power and Satisfaction in Marriage: A Review and Critique," *Psychological Bulletin* 93 (1983): 513–538.

18. For more about the problem with focusing on self-esteem, see R. Dawes, "The Social Usefulness of Self Esteem: A Skeptical View," *Harvard Mental Health Letter* (October 1998): 4–5.

19. For a scientific analysis of love, see Helen Fischer's excellent review of the topic in *Anatomy of Love: The Natural History of Monogamy, Adultery, and Divorce* (New York: W. W. Norton, 1992).

20. S. Murray, "The Quest for Conviction: Motivated Cognition in Romantic Relationships," *Psychological Inquiry* 10 (1999): 23–34.

21. Martin Seligman, *Authentic Happiness: Using the New Positive Psychology to Realize Your Potential for Lasting Fulfillment* (New York: Free Press, 2003), 200.

Chapter 6. Committed to a Family Asylum

1. For a description of this classic work, see H. Harlow, "The Nature of Love," *American Psychologist* 13 (1958).

2. R. Plomin and D. Daniels, "Why Are Children in the Same Family So Different from One Another?" *Behavioral and Brain Sciences* 10 (1987): 1–60.

3. M. S. Gazzaniga, *Nature's Mind: The Biological Roots of Thinking, Emotions, Sexuality, Language, and Intelligence* (New York: Basic Books, 1992), 202.

4. M. E. P. Seligman, *What You Can Change and What You Can't* (New York: Knopf, 1994), 87.

5. A. Pope, from Bartlett's *Familiar Quotations,* 230. W. Wordworth's quote is from "My Heart Leaps Up When I Behold," in Bartlett's *Familiar Quotations,* 469. Robyn M. Dawes traces this idea of our "twiggish" nature back to these ideas and documents how wrong the assumption is in her excellent *House of Cards: Psychology and Psychotherapy Built on Myth* (New York: Free Press, 1994). I consider this decade-old book to be required reading for anyone interested in genuine mindful self-help and, particularly, as Dawes points out, the almost two-thirds of psychologists who don't read scientific journals.

6. R. M. Dawes, *House of Cards: Psychology and Psychotherapy Built on Myth* (New York: Free Press, 1994), 218.

7. As quoted in C. L. M. Keyes, "Complete Mental Health: An Agenda for the 21st Century," in *Flourishing: Positive Psychology and the Life Well-Lived,* ed. C. L. M. Keyes and J. Haidt (Washington, D.C.: American Psychological Association, 2003), 293–312.

8. See L. G. Russek and G. E. Schwartz, "Narrative Descriptions of Parental Love and Caring Predict Health Status in Midlife: A 35-Year Follow-Up of the Harvard Mastery of Stress Study," *Alternative Therapies* 2 (1996): 53–62.

9. D. G. Myers, *The American Paradox* (New Haven, Conn.: Yale University Press, 2000), 42.

10. Some of this research is summarized in J. Leo, "The Sleeper Effect," *U.S. News & World Report* (October 2000): 18. See also H. S. Friedman et al., "Psychological and Behavioral Predictors of Longevity," *American Psychologist* 50, no. 2 (1995): 69–78.

11. E. S. Werner and R. S. Smith, *Vulnerable but Invincible: A Study of Resilient Children* (New York: McGraw Hill, 1982). See also Werner and Smith's work following up on their initial study as published in *High Risk Children from Birth to Adulthood* (Ithaca, N.Y.: Cornell University Press, 1992).

12. S. Scarr, D. Phillips, and K. McCartney, "Facts, Fantasies, and the Future of Child Care in the United States," *Psychological Science* 1 (1990): 26–33. See also S. Scarr and J. Arnett, "Malleability: Lessons from Intervention and Family Studies," in *The Malleability of Children,* ed. J. J. Gallagher (New York: Basic Books, 1987), 71–84. See also J. Kagan, "Family Experience and the Child's Development," *American Psychologist* 34 (1979): 886–891.

13. C. S. Widom, "The Cycle of Violence," *Science* 244 (1989): 160–166.

14. Ibid., 162.

15. Ibid., 163.

16. P. B. Neubaurer and A. Neubauer, *Nature's Thumbprint: The New Genetics of Personality* (Reading, Mass.: Addison-Wesley, 1990), 20–21.

17. As reported in J. Collier, *The Rise of Selfishness in America* (Oxford, U.K.: Oxford University Press, 1991).

18. R. Baumeister, "Should Schools Try to Boost Self-Esteem? Beware the Dark Side," *American Educator* 20 (1996): 14–19.

19. R. Dawes, "The Social Usefulness of Self-Esteem: A Skeptical View," *Harvard Mental Health Letter* (October 1998): 4–5.

Chapter 7. A Lively Livelihood

1. J. DeGraaf, D. Wann, and T. H. Naylor, *Affluenza: The All-Consuming Epidemic* (San Francisco: Berrett-Koehler, 2001), 2.

2. This work is described in my book *Toxic Success: How to Stop Striving and Start Thriving* (Makawau, Hawaii: Inner Ocean Publishing, 2002). See also P. Pearsall, "Toxic Success and the Mind of a Surgeon," *Archives of Surgery* 139 (2004): 879–888.

3. R. A. Emmons, "Personal Goals, Life Meaning, and Virtue: Wellsprings of a Positive Life," in *Flourishing: Positive Psychology and the Life Well-Lived,* ed.

C. L. M. Keyes and J. Haidt (Washington, D.C.: American Psychological Association, 2003), 105–128.

4. As reported in R. Nilsen, "Take It Slow," *Honolulu Advertiser,* August 31, 2003, E10.

5. R. M. Sapolsky, *Why Zebras Don't Get Ulcers* (New York: W. H. Freeman, 1994), 55.

6. M. Friedman and R. H. Rosenman, *Type A Behavior and Your Heart* (New York: Knopf, 1974), 4.

7. J. Gleick, *Faster: The Acceleration of Just About Everything* (New York: Pantheon, 1999), 17.

8. T. Kamark and J. R. Jennings, "Biobehavioral Factors in Sudden Cardiac Death," *Psychological Bulletin* 109 (1991): 42–75.

9. As descried in T. Ferguson, "Contented Workaholics," *Medical Self-Care* (1981): 20–24.

10. Sir Laurens van der Post, *Jung and the Story of Our Time* (New York: Random House/Vintage, 1977), 76–77.

11. The psychologist Mihaly Csikszentmihalyi coined the word "flow" and did extensive research in the idea of the joy of total loss of awareness of self. See Mihaly Csikzentmihalyi, *The Psychology of Optimal Experience* (New York: Harper & Row, 1990). This is another example of an excellent scientifically based creative self-help book.

Chapter 8. Escape from Health Hysteria

1. This origin of the word "health" is described by the health psychologist Richard Straub, *Health Psychology* (New York: Worth, 2002), 6.

2. This example is taken from Norman B. Anderson and P. Elizabeth Anderson, *Emotional Longevity* (New York: Viking, 2003), 150, an excellent book about health and longevity. This is another example of a scientific creative self-help book and I highly recommend it.

3. J. Smith, "Healthy Bodies and Thick Wallets: The Dual Relation Between Health and Socioeconomic Status," *Journal of Economic Perspectives* 10 (1999): 145–166.

4. These findings are from a German study published in the *Journal of the American Medical Association.* As reported in L. Tanner, "Eating Dark Chocolate Just Got a Little Less Sinful," *Honolulu Advertiser,* August 27, 2003.

5. As reported in E. C. Reynolds, "The Prevention of Sub-Surface Demineralization of Bovine Enamel and Change in Plaque Composition by Casein in an Intro-Oral Model," *Journal of Dental Research* 66, no. 6 (1985): 1120–1127.

6. For a discussion of some of the "false risk factors," see R. Ornstein and D. Sobel, *Healthy Pleasures* (Reading, Mass.: Addison-Wesley, 1989).

7. At the time of this writing, this study has not yet been published. I became aware of it while a clinical adjunct professor at the University of Hawaii at Manoa.

8. As quoted in E. B. Holifield, *A History of Pastoral Care in America* (Nashville, Tenn.: Abingdon Press, 1983), 209.

9. S. Breznitz, "The Noble Challenge of Stress," in *Stress in Israel,* ed. S. Breznitz (New York: Van Nostrand Reinhold, 1983), 265.

10. P. Pearsall, *The Beethoven Factor: The New Positive Psychology of Hardiness, Happiness, Healing, and Hope* (Charlottesville, Va.: Hampton Roads, 2003).

11. E. J. Ozer et al., "Predictors of Posttraumatic Stress Disorder and Symptoms in Adults: A Meta-analysis," *Psychological Bulletin* 129 (2003): 52–71.

12. G. A. Bonanno, "Loss, Trauma, and Human Resilience: Have We Underestimated the Human Capacity to Thrive After Extremely Aversive Events?" *American Psychologist* (January 2004): 20.

13. E. S. Fisher and H. G. Welch, "Avoiding the Unintended Consequences of Growth in Medical Care: How More Might Be Worse," *Journal of the American Medical Association* 81, no. 5 (1999): 445–453.

14. C. K. Meador, "The Last Well Person," *New England Journal of Medicine* 330, no. 6 (1994): 440–441.

15. R. M. Nesse and G. C. Williams, *Why We Get Sick: The New Science of Darwinian Medicine* (New York: Random House, 1994).

16. For more information about craving, habituation, and refraction, see P. Shizgal, "Neural Basis of Utility Estimation," *Current Opinion in Neurobiology* 7 (1997): 198–208.

17. J. K. Norem, *The Positive Power of Negative Thinking* (New York: Basic Books, 2001).

18. S. Segerstrom et al., "Optimism Is Associated with Mood, Coping, and Immune Change in Response to Stress," *Journal of Personality and Social Psychology* 74 (1998): 1646–1655.

19. The paradox of the healing power of surrender is discussed by B. S. Cole and K. I. Pargament in "Spiritual Surrender: A Paradoxical Path to Control," in *Integrating Spirituality Into Treatment: Resources for Practitioners,* ed. W. R. Miller (Washington, D.C.: American Psychological Association, 1999), 179–198.

20. For a description of this trapped state and its emotional consequences, see C. S. Carver and M. F. Scheier, "Origins and Functions of Positive and Negative Affect: A Control-Process View," *Psychological Review* 97 (1990): 19–35.

Chapter 9. Overcoming the Burden of Youth

1. Our life span is increasing, but the optimal life span remains at about 115 to 120 years. For a discussion of our biological living potential, see W. M. Bortz, *We Live Too Short and Die Too Long: How to Achieve Your Natural 100-Year-Plus Life Span* (New York: Bantam, 1992).

2. Ibid. See also Bortz's "The Oldest Old," *Scientific American* (January 1995): 70–75.

3. For an excellent presentation of statistics regarding aging, see A. Pife and L. Bronte, *Our Aging Society* (New York: Norton, 1986).

4. W. A. Sadler, *The Third Age: 6 Principles for Growth and Renewal After Forty* (Cambridge, Mass.: Perseus, 2000), 18.

5. J. M. Rybash, P. A. Roodin, and W. J. Hoyer, *Adult Development and Aging* (Madison, Wis.: Brown and Benchmark, 1995).

6. For more information about the health of seniors, see G. M. Williamson, "Aging Well," in *Handbook of Positive Psychology,* ed. C. R. Snyder and S. J. Lopez (New York: Oxford University Press, 2002), 676–686.

7. K. G. Manton, E. Stallard, and L. Corder, "Changes in Morbidity and Chronic Disability in the U.S. Elderly Population: Evidence from the 1982, 1984, and 1999 National Long-Term Care Surveys," *Journal of Gerontology* 50 (1995): 1914–204.

8. Williamson, "Aging Well," 677.

9. M. P. Lawton and L. Nahemow, "Ecology and the Aging Process," in *Psychology of Adult Development and Aging,* ed. C. Eisdorger and M. P. Lawton (Washington, D.C.: American Psychological Association, 1973), 619–674.

Chapter 10. Healthy Dying and Good Grieving

1. See A. Calaprice, ed., *Dear Professor Einstein* (New York: Barnes and Noble Books, 2002), 181–184.

2. Ibid., 183.

3. C. G. Davis, S. Nolen-Hoeksema, and J. Larson, "Making Sense of Loss and Benefiting from the Experience: Two Constructs of Meaning," *Journal of Personality and Social Psychology* 75 (1998): 561–574.

4. D. Wegner, *White Bears and Other Unwanted Things* (New York: Guilford Publishers, 1994). For an interesting presentation regarding the issue of "free will" and whether we can really follow self-helpism's advice and "think it and make it happen," see D. M. Wegner, "When the Antidote Is the Poison: Ironic Mental Control Processes," *Psychological Science* 8 (1997): 148–150.

5. E. de Bono, *I Am Right, You Are Wrong: From Rock Logic to Water Logic* (New York: Viking, 1991).

6. This astonishing research is described in T. Shroder, *Old Souls: The Scientific Evidence for Past Lives* (New York: Simon & Schuster, 1999).

7. G. A. Bonanno, "Loss, Trauma, and Human Resilience," *American Psychologist* (January 2004): 20–27.

8. G. A. Bonanno and S. Kaltman, "The Varieties of Grief Experience," *Clinical Psychology Review* 125 (1999): 760–776.

Epilogue. The Fifth Factor

1. For a more detailed description of these factors, see R. R. McCrae and P. T. Costa, Jr., "Validation of a Five-Factor Model of Personality Across Instruments and Observers," *Journal of Personality and Social Psychology* 52 (1987): 81–90.

2. K. Kersting, "Turning Happiness Into Economic Power," *Monitor on Psychology* (December 2003): 27.

3. A version of Perls's prayer appears in D. G. Meyers, *The American Paradox: Spiritual Hunger in an Age of Plenty* (New Haven, Conn.: Yale University Press, 2000), 168.

Index